LOVING A BIPOLAR BEAR

LOVING A BIPOLAR BEAR

JANELL BORRERO PEÑA

NEW DEGREE PRESS
COPYRIGHT © 2023 JANELL BORRERO PEÑA
All rights reserved.

LOVING A BIPOLAR BEAR

ISBN   979-8-88926-605-1 *Paperback*
         979-8-88926-607-5 *Hardcover*
         979-8-88926-606-8 *Ebook*

CONTENTS

INTRODUCTION 7

CHAPTER 1. HISTORY 13
CHAPTER 2. BIRTHDAY SURPRISE 23
CHAPTER 3. NO TURNING BACK 33
CHAPTER 4. THE NEXT DAY 43
CHAPTER 5. MY JOURNEY 51
CHAPTER 6. THE BEGINNING 59
CHAPTER 7. SUMMER NEVER ENDED 71
CHAPTER 8. IN SICKNESS AND IN HEALTH 83
CHAPTER 9. OVERDOSE 93
CHAPTER 10. DISCHARGE 107
CHAPTER 11. BAKER ACT 115
CHAPTER 12. INTROVERT OR NOT 125
CHAPTER 13. SHOOTING 133
CHAPTER 14. THIRTY-EIGHT 145
CHAPTER 15. RESENTMENT 157
CHAPTER 16. I DID IT AGAIN 167
CHAPTER 17. MY PUNISHMENT 175
CHAPTER 18. YOU ARE NOT ALONE 187
CHAPTER 19. THE FINAL CHAPTER 199

ACKNOWLEDGMENTS 209
APPENDIX 211

INTRODUCTION

"Janell, I think the best thing for us is to go our separate ways."

On January 20, 2022, the person I loved for seventeen years said those words to me. The person I tried my hardest never to give up on turned around and gave up on me. As the saying goes, a young lady marries a man that reminds them of their father. When I met Carlos, I couldn't disagree or agree with the father part because mine wasn't around. My mother was the only parent present throughout my formative years.

Her struggles with mental illness caused her to behave in ways that influenced my tolerance and compassion for actions that were not normal. So, when I chose a partner for life, I found someone who would not abandon me like my father—or so I thought. I didn't know I was choosing someone battling a mental illness just like my mother. So, I guess I did match my parents.

I did believe that once I got married, the marriage was forever. I took the vows for better or for worse very seriously, but for better or for worse shouldn't have been at the cost of my mental sanity.

I've come to believe it doesn't matter how much work you put into a relationship or any individual. They will never change unless they want to change for themselves. Throw mental illness into the mix, making it much harder.

After so many therapy sessions, self-help books, magazine articles, and damn near just giving up on myself, I've realized I'm not responsible for someone else's actions, just my own. Their negativity does not reflect the type of person I am or was. We can only control ourselves and how we respond, overcome, and grow.

If the best thing for you and your happiness is to walk away, you should do so and not feel like a failure in choosing yourself. I was always afraid to end our relationship. The biggest fear was that Carlos would take his own life. These were the questions I would let run through my mind.

How can anyone leave their spouse when they are in need?

How can anyone walk away in this time of sickness?

Would he be able to manage me leaving him?

The fear did come along because I did experience several suicides in my family. That guilt for me was so intense, but after years of battling that guilt, he made the decision himself and walked away from me. He turned the negativity onto me as if I were the problem. He had a fantastic way of showing appreciation for someone who had been by his side for so much.

"You aren't supportive or genuine, you fear my growth, and I feel you are trying to have a baby with me to keep me." These were the last words Carlos used to describe me.

I'm not writing this book to bash anyone. I'm writing this book because there are many individuals in the world living with and loving someone with a mental illness. Mental illness isn't uncomplicated for those diagnosed with the disorder, but people forget about those living with them and loving them.

I wanted to write this book to express my sadness, frustrations, compassion, hurt, and love for those who were or currently are in my life with a mental illness. I wanted to show a positive side to someone with mental illness. Not everyone has experience handling such struggles and has never experienced love from the same person.

I want to be honest and not sugarcoat anything that has transpired throughout all these years. This book will be the raw version of how dealing with someone diagnosed and undiagnosed with a mental illness can affect their loved ones. I also want everyone to understand why I've held on for so long and never wanted to give up.

There are many books on treating mental illness or the definition of different mental illnesses, but I haven't found a book with a voice like mine. My voice with tears in my eyes, sharing many situations that transpired but still holding no grudges toward anyone. I don't blame them because they didn't choose to have a mental illness, but these mental illnesses have, in their way, defined us.

This book is my journey of how I learned to deal with the instabilities of mental illness that eventually led to a seventeen-year relationship with someone with similar traits. These mental illnesses can cause loved one's insecurities, self-doubt, depression, anxiety, and hypersensitivity, creating an ultimate empath.

We love our loved ones so much that we protect them from the world, and we don't want to seek help for what is going on without realizing that we are drowning. The guilt we carry in our hearts if we say *no* to a mentally ill loved one may cause them to hurt themselves, which keeps us from moving on or standing our ground.

I hope this book lets you know you are not alone on this journey. It isn't your fault your loved one is ill, but we must regain our power healthily. Choose yourself first because if no one is taking care of you, you won't have anything to give to the rest of the world later.

This book will be for anyone who can relate to growing up with parents, living with a spouse, or living with a loved one diagnosed with a mental illness. To see how going from a caring individual can lead up to someone who sounds straight cold-hearted because you are tired.

I had a very rough upbringing where there was mental and physical abuse. Later, I dealt with a sick spouse. Despite these challenges, I've used what I learned to become the person and entrepreneur I am today. You will understand some steps I've tried using to help be at peace before, during, and after my relationship ended. Healing is ongoing, so I'm forever learning. I am currently on the journey to finding myself again.

CHAPTER 1

HISTORY

"A person living with a mental illness could never be normal."

I've heard this statement many times, and I felt it was true until I put the work in to understand and empathize with those suffering. To get started, let me describe what a mental disorder is by definition. A mental illness is a wide range of conditions that affect mood, thinking, feeling, and behavior (National Alliance of Mental Health, n.d.).

A wide range of conditions falls under the mental disorder category. Clinical depression, anxiety disorder, dementia, attention deficit hyperactivity disorder, schizophrenia, obsessive-compulsive disorder, autism, and post-traumatic stress disorder are the most common. Here are some statistics I pulled from nami.org (National Alliance of Mental Health, n.d.):

> One in five US adults experiences mental illness each year.

> One in twenty US adults experiences
> serious mental illness each year.
> One in six youths aged six to seventeen
> experience a mental health disorder each year.
> Fifty percent of all mental illness begins by age
> fourteen and 75 percent by age twenty-four.

Yes, someone with a mental illness can live a simple everyday life. But this book isn't going to be about the scientific aspect but about the effects that mental illnesses can have on a loved one or caregiver.

I will walk you through my experiences with my family members, by blood or marriage, since I was a child and all through my adult years. I have also interviewed other individuals who have a mental disorder or are currently dealing with someone who suffers/suffered from a mental illness.

I want to warn you that these stories may trigger something in you if you suffer from similar experiences, or it may shock you at what I've had to deal with in the past.

I didn't want to write this book to give you some interesting stories but also to help identify the different emotions I've felt during my experiences. So, I will point out the other feelings or the lack of emotions I didn't think about while going through some traumatic events. While conducting interviews and talking to others about this book, I understood that many people in my shoes experienced something similar, which meant I was not alone.

I want you to realize you are not alone, either.

I also want to provide different resources I've used throughout these years to keep me sane and educated. From websites I've used as my research resource to other counselors I've spoken with during hard times.

I will also explain how I tried to stay on a positive path throughout these years. Dealing with mental illness isn't easy, but I've played it off very well. I may have just been playing a role I knew how to play for so long.

I'm not saying I didn't love my family because I love them with all my heart and would still do anything for them, but now with boundaries.

I am no pro at doing great all the time and believe me, I've had my fair share of fuck ups along the way, but I've kept them a secret solely to protect the feelings of others. Now I no longer have to save anyone but myself. I can directly speak my entire truth without the fear of any backlash.

My first experience with a mental disorder was with my mother. As far back as I can remember, my mother battled something, but she has never admitted it. We all just learned to excuse her behavior and move on.

My mother educated herself about mental illness because her younger brother had schizophrenia since he was a child. She was aware of his condition and did everything to help him, but when it came to her, she ignored it.

To this day, I am not even sure if she ever received a formal diagnosis from a doctor. She refuses to see doctors even if she has a fever. I think the only time I have seen her in the hospital or doctor's office was when she was pregnant with my younger siblings.

My other experience was with my uncle. I experienced his behavioral changes at a young age, and I didn't understand why he was such a loner. There were times he came around and loved us so much, but there were times he hated us all. He would always tell me I was his favorite, but honestly, he would say that to each of his nieces.

One day he scared me so much. I was about thirteen years old, and he came to our home. He needed money for his alcohol and was asking my mother. My mother had no money, so he turned and looked at me. He remembered he had found a ring and given it to me years prior. He asked for the piece of jewelry back, and I told him I did not have it, which was true. But he didn't believe me and became furious.

I was sitting on a rocking chair. My uncle Joe stepped right in front of me, so angry that I felt I was looking at the devil. He leaned over me and pushed the chair back so my feet dangled. I kept telling him to back off, but he had such anger that he couldn't hear me. So, I was calm the entire time.

My mother said his name once, "*Joe,*" and he moved. She told him he couldn't do that.

He said, "Okay." My uncle then left calmly. It was like her tone of voice was so familiar to him, and he respected her. He did not even talk back. She had a power that amazed me.

Seeing their interactions was fascinating. They were just a year apart, with my mother being the oldest. From my understanding, she took the role of taking care of him. She knew exactly how to deal with him and how to identify when she couldn't deal with him. Unfortunately, in my early twenties, he passed away from hypothermia. He was drinking and fell asleep outside, which we all feared would happen. It was a sad moment for all of us, but as my grandmother said, he is no longer suffering.

On June 12, 2004, I received a phone call that my younger cousin had taken her own life. I knew she battled with depression, but I would have never thought she would take her own life. When I received the phone call, I couldn't believe it, and to this day, I ask myself why. I don't talk about her much but believe me when I say we were more than cousins. We were siblings, and I miss her dearly. I ignored her passing for a long time until the next traumatic event happened, and I had no choice but to mourn her.

On June 3, 2005, I received a phone call that my uncle, which biologically was my mother's cousin, had taken his life. Again, depression was an ongoing battle for him for many years. I knew what he battled, and having my cousin, his biological cousin, take her life triggered something in him. There were other factors I won't state here because it isn't my story to share. But his death made me stop everything in life and mourn him and my cousin.

That summer, I met Carlos. It was an ongoing joke that he was my summer fling. I honestly didn't expect anything from him other than company during my sadness.

Years later, on March 11, 2010, I received another phone call that my stepmother had passed away. She accidentally overdosed on her medication. Afterward, I didn't speak to my dad much because she was the one that maintained our relationship. I remember being angry because I saw her battle with addiction to prescription medication, but I never thought those pills would end her life.

Years later, yet again, another phone call. This time, it was regarding my husband.

"Baby, did you know I was diagnosed with manic depressive disorder and borderline personality disorder?" he asked me.

"No, what is that?" I said, confused.

I honestly had no clue what any of that meant. Carlos's diagnosis was sometime in 2009 before we got married, all while he was recovering from an injury. While working for Costco, Carlos had an accident. He was lifting a pallet of bananas which forever changed our lives. He injured the L4, L5, and S1 discs in his spine. Several surgeries later, we still battled the consequences.

I researched what these diagnoses were because I was inquisitive. Manic depressive disorder is another way of saying bipolar disorder. That freaked me out.

By definition, bipolar disorder is a disorder associated with episodes of mood swings ranging from depressive lows to manic highs (National Alliance of Mental Health n.d.). Symptoms include high energy, reduced need for sleep, and loss of touch with reality. Depressive episodes may include low energy, low motivation, and decreased interest in daily activities.

I spent countless hours trying to educate myself on this disorder, but I forgot about his second diagnosis for a while. Borderline personality was something I had never heard of before, so I dove into my research.

Borderline personality disorder is a mental disorder characterized by unstable moods, behavior, and relationships. Symptoms include emotional instability, worthlessness, insecurity, impulsivity, and impaired social relationships.

From my understanding, Carlos had these disorders since he was young but displayed no symptoms until after his injury. He, his father, and I received a large packet of questionnaires from the Social Security Administration to fill out. There were questions about everything from his sleep to money, sex, and hobbies. In addition, there were detailed questions we were confused about because we had thought this was about his back. But low and behold, they were worried about his mental health, and he qualified for Social Security benefits.

Now, for my diagnosis, I knew something was not right with me and my body for many years. I would go for months without my menstrual cycle, I gained weight by smelling food, I had issues sleeping, I had problems waking up in the morning, I had hair growing in places that should not be on a female, and I had depression and anxiety. I blamed my depression and anxiety on the environment, but I did not realize it was also related to my diagnosis.

My ob-gyn ran blood work and ultrasounds to conclude that I had PCOS. PCOS is polycystic ovary syndrome, a hormonal disorder causing enlarged ovaries with small cysts on the outer edges. It didn't affect my ovaries but caused so many issues for me. Stress was a major trigger for my PCOS not being controllable.

I've designed this book to shed light on the difficulties mental disorders can have on the family and loved ones. Relationships can get ruined when both parties do not seek help, not just the diagnosed.

I want people to understand the struggle when you love someone so much that you subconsciously become an enabler. Once you become an enabler, it is not easy to stop. Many will judge you and quickly criticize you for what you have done or the lack of but know that no one can tell you what you should or should not do if they are not you.

Shit, I could only tell you what I wish I could have done differently now that I'm looking back, but at those moments, I did what I thought was best. I'm speaking from experience and providing tips for you to stop being an enabler and put yourself first.

When I spoke to my counselor about this book, her reply was, "Janell, this book will be great because there isn't anything like it. We have books on symptoms and how we suggest handling but nothing from the family." Those words encouraged me. We closed our session with her saying, "I could only provide recommendations, but at the end of the day, I don't live with you to know exactly how you feel. You have to do what's best for you."

So here we are, I've written a book, and you are about to enter my world. The world I so anxiously hid from so many people is all on paper—no more running and hiding behind a fake smile. Now you will see who hurt me and how they hurt me. You will also witness who has left my life and who has stayed. Then, a decision changed my life forever.

I lost myself while I was trying to figure out someone else. I was in a profound depression, and I wasn't aware. As much as I would love to help instruct you down the correct path to recovery, I just cannot. I'm still trying to figure it all out for myself. My intention when I started writing this book was to help heal myself. While researching, I saw a TikTok video of an individual speaking about healing. He talked about the book *Love after Heartbreak* (Labossiere 2019). I rushed to order it because I was desperate for healing.

In the book, he suggested writing a letter to all those who have hurt me (Labossiere 2019). So, I wrote the first letter to my mother and then to Carlos. Initially, I wanted to share these journal entries so you could understand my pain, anger, and emotions. However, I decided it would be better to write an entire book about it.

CHAPTER 2

BIRTHDAY SURPRISE

What is the difference between a fifteen-year-old versus a sixteen-year-old? If you guessed sixteen-year-olds could get a job, then you are correct. Hallufuckingllujah! The excitement I felt when I turned sixteen. All the butterflies I had the last night of being fifteen continued into the morning of my sixteenth birthday. I smiled and felt my entire body shiver.

Yes! Dammit! Yes! I'm finally sixteen years old. It may not be a big deal to you that I had just turned sixteen, or maybe you're confused about why I was so excited. I couldn't drink or purchase cigarettes, so what was all the fuss about turning sixteen? Before I explain why I was so excited, I have to walk you through my day.

I was lying in bed and thinking about all the possibilities that would come along for me now that I was the big sixteen. I was the best at daydreaming, which was what I started to do. My mind started shifting away to daydreaming about all the positive outcomes, which just motivated me. I stared straight up at my five-by-ten small bedroom ceiling. Well, technically, my room was an enclosed porch that I made into my bedroom so I wouldn't have to continue sharing a room with my twenty-year-old brother.

It was a Saturday in November, so it was cold in my room. I had been sixteen for two whole days at this point. While still in bed, I reached over to open my door to let the heat from the kitchen flow into my bedroom. I waited several minutes for the warmth to go through my body. Finally, the heat kicked on, and I jumped out of bed with excitement and started looking for clothes to wear.

I opened and closed my drawers, trying to find a perfect outfit. But unfortunately, I only had a few clothes to choose from, so I stood there looking over my limited options.

"I can't wait to be able to buy my things, so I don't have to worry about this again," I said. I tried matching a pair of jeans with a long sleeve T-shirt and some gym shoes. I ensured it would be warm enough to withstand the cold while standing to wait for public transportation.

The clothes I picked out would have to do for now because there wasn't anything else I could put together. I grabbed everything and walked through the kitchen, past my mother's room, and to our bathroom. I turned on the shower to let it warm up before jumping in. I closed the door behind me. Before I even started getting undressed, my mother started walking toward the bathroom, so I waited. I stood there waiting for words to come out of her mouth.

"What are you doing?" my mother barked.

"I'm getting ready to go downtown to apply for jobs," I responded loud enough so she could hear over the water running. I was excited because I was of legal age to find a job.

I waited a few seconds to hear a response from her, but it was silent. I tried to feel the energy to know how I should act with her once I got out of the bathroom. My body tensed up, waiting for a response, but I didn't hear anything from the other side of the door, so all was clear. I proceeded to get undressed, and I jumped in the shower quickly. My friend was on the way, so I wanted to make sure I was out before she got to our apartment.

The doorbell rang, and I knew it had to be Enelise. So, I jumped out of the shower and dressed quickly. Once dressed, I grabbed all my stuff from the bathroom floor and took it to my bedroom. I threw my pajamas into my laundry pile and grabbed my coat to head out the door.

I quickly walked through the kitchen past my mother's room, hoping I could avoid seeing her. Then, I heard her voice again asking, "Where are you going?" but this time, she was much closer to me.

I turned to see her staring straight into my face and said, "I told you I was going downtown to apply for jobs."

"Dressed like that and on a Saturday?" She looked at me with disgust written all over her face.

I didn't see anything wrong with what I was wearing. I had a white cotton shirt with a collar, jeans with no rips, and a pair of clean gym shoes. Yes, gym shoes. For those of you that don't understand what gym shoes are, I will translate them for you. Gym shoes are how we Midwesterners say, kicks or sneakers. Unfortunately, I didn't even get a chance to respond.

I didn't see it coming, but my mother's right hand struck my face. Her hand hit me in my right eye, followed up by a quick left hook to my left eye. I placed my hands over my face and bent over as quickly as possible without moving or running away. I put my hands over my eyes so she couldn't do much damage. The palm of my hands was over my eyes, with the lower palm where it meets the wrist falling right under the eye socket.

"I'm not stupid," she yelled while continuing to strike my face. "I know you guys are going to be whores and look for boys."

I didn't dare speak back to her. There was no way for me to convince my mother I wasn't looking for boys. My mother would create these wild stories in her head and believe them no matter what I told her. I never understood why her go-to story was me with boys. I just knew I had to stay bent over and protect myself. I kept both hands over my eyes, hoping she just got tired. But, with every strike, I saw moons and stars. Not one tear came out of my eyes, and if I tried crying, she would have slapped them right back into my eye socket.

I kept my composure while she finished letting out her aggression. I didn't even attempt to move from the spot she caught me. If I did, it was just going to make matters worse. So, I stood there, taking every hit she was giving. I didn't feel any of it. I knew she was hitting me because I kept seeing what looked like stars, but I honestly didn't feel it. The lightning strikes kept getting brighter, but I didn't feel it. I felt like I was watching what was going on as if I was a third persona, and it wasn't happening to me.

I no longer saw the image of lightning as I slowly took my hands away from my face to look up. My mother was standing right before me, just waiting for me to do or say something.

With a sound of authority and no fear, I looked her dead in the eyes and said, "I'll be back." I couldn't show her that she affected me in any way. I walked past the dining room into the living room, where Enelise stood in disbelief at what she had just witnessed.

"If you are leaving my house, you better leave my keys here," my mother shouted.

I knew my mother was upset because she didn't get the outcome she expected from me. This ass-whooping was a way to manipulate me into staying and not looking for employment. But I needed her to understand she couldn't control me. I needed to get a job no matter how she felt about me possibly succeeding in life. So, I turned around and walked back to the dining room.

I threw my keys onto the dining room table. "Here you go," I said back to her calmly. I looked at Enelise and said, "Come on," as if nothing had happened.

Enelise and I walked down Augusta, the main street where I lived, and turned right on the side road that led to the bus stop. I walked up to a parked car to use the mirror to look at my face. Unfortunately, it was so cold outside that the mirror was frosty, preventing me from having a clear view. Nevertheless, what I did see wasn't a surprise.

Both eyes had half a ring of busted blood vessels underneath. It looked like half a moon facing upward. It bruised entirely, but I could see the injured tiny blood vessels. I guess from me blocking my eyes, she could only hit the back of my hands, but the force of her hit caused me to inflict injury upon my face. My hands protected me from having full-blown black and blue eyes, for which I was lucky, but now I was walking around with a different type of injury.

"Okay, it isn't so bad." I kept walking.

We walked to the bus stop, and neither of us said a word. Enelise wouldn't look at me to avoid having to give me any facial reactions. We waited about twenty minutes for the bus and spent another thirty minutes on the bus to get to our destination.

I applied to a movie theater opening in the next several weeks. However, after the embarrassing moment of submitting applications with a bruised face, I felt I couldn't bear another awkward moment, so I decided not to continue my job search.

"Lord, please let me get this job because I need a way out," I said to myself with a desperate feeling flowing through my body. I knew I would die in my mother's hands one day if I didn't get out. So, I looked at Enelise and told her I didn't want to apply for anything else.

"Okay," she replied.

We walked down to the Nike Store in Downtown Chicago. I had never been there before, so it took my mind off things for several hours until I felt like going back home.

Several hours passed, and knowing my mother, she hadn't calmed down yet. I knew she would feel like she had unfinished business. The fact that I still left would make her think she had no control over me. Enelise and I jumped back onto the bus for the thirty-minute ride home. We walked back to the apartment. I saw all the lights were off. I figured she went to sleep so she didn't have to let me into the apartment.

It was cold outside, and I didn't know what to do. Enelise wouldn't leave me alone, and I wouldn't stay at her house. If I rang the doorbell, it would cause something else between my mother and me, but if I had stayed over at Enelise's house, my mother would have justified her made-up story and caused a different issue.

Either way, I was screwed. I just had to figure out what would be the least impactful. So, I stood on the top of my front porch looking around, confused and not knowing where to go.

Enelise suggested, "Why don't we go across to street to Victor's apartment? I'm sure the guys are there right now."

Victor was a friend of both of our brothers. My brother, Noel, always told me I was forbidden to step foot into that apartment. One reason was that most of the time, it was just guys, and the other was because of the illegal activities that would take place.

He never wanted me involved in that situation, but at this point, I couldn't feel my fingers. So, I had to give it a chance to see if my brother was there.

"Okay, but if Noel gets mad at me, we are out of that apartment fast," I responded to her.

They had already seen us coming and walked up the back stairs since cameras were all around the building for their protection. My brother didn't even wait until I got to the door to open it and questioned why I was there in the first place. I didn't have to explain anything to him once he looked at my face. He led me into the apartment and told me not to move. He went in and got his coat.

"Come on," he said.

We walked across the street. Noel opened the door without any hesitation and walked right behind me. My mother exited her room into the hallway and questioned why I was in her house. My brother told her he had let me in and that I would stay in the apartment. She turned around, mumbling something about us thinking we ruled her home.

I walked straight to my room. I walked past my mother's room door as if I had blinders on the side of my face. I didn't look to see where she was, and I didn't say a word. It was easier to pretend I didn't see her, but I needed to be cautious because I didn't know her next move. Since she was unpredictable, I decided to keep my clothes on. I just lay on the bed and threw the blankets over me.

I lay on the bed for several hours in silence, thinking about all the opportunities I would have if I were to get hired. I played different scenarios in my head on what I would do if I started making my own money. What would be the first thing I would buy? Would I save money to move out? The possibilities were endless, but I kept playing with the scenarios until I closed my eyes and fell asleep.

CHAPTER 3

NO TURNING BACK

Yes, I did get the job at the movie theater.

It excited me that I could now enjoy my own money. I had to pay my mother $50 from each paycheck to contribute to the household. That was my form of rent which was my mother's way of teaching me responsibilities.

Despite having my job, the best job is being a nonpaid babysitter without even asking for the job. The appointed position was mine to keep since I was the eldest female. The oldest of us four was my brother, who was four years older than me and a male, so that surely wasn't going to be his job.

"Your uncle is going to pick me up, and you need to take care of the kids," my mother said in her demanding voice. She is very stern and doesn't show much emotion to anyone. She seems to always be mad at the world, and if you get her to laugh, it's a rare moment that needs to be captured with pictures to believe it even happened. This particular day she was heading out to a family member's home since her uncle, my maternal grandmother's brother, passed away earlier that day.

"By the time I return, you better have fed them, bathed them, and put them in bed," she continued demanding of me. At sixteen years old, there were other things I could think of doing than taking care of two toddlers. Don't get me wrong, I loved my little siblings, but they were not my responsibility. I knew not to object to her demands. Although my mother didn't show her emotions in the natural, usual way of ugly crying when someone passes away, she showed her emotions with anger toward the world.

She leaves the apartment, and now I'm in charge of mom duties. About six hours passed, and I fed Joey and Sammy. They were playing in the shared crib, and I knew it was time for a bath so they could get to sleep. So, I walked to the bathroom across the hall from my mother's bedroom. I heard one of their voices say "Nell," but how they pronounced it was similar to a cat meowing.

"*Nell*," for the second time, means I need to hurry.

I chuckled because they didn't have me in their eyesight and needed to see me. But I had to hurry because Sammy dared to throw herself out of the crib to find me. It would never fail, so I needed to ensure I got them out of the crib before she threw herself.

I turned the water on in the tub and made sure the water was warm. Then, I grabbed the soap container to pour the soap into the water. Joey and Sammy always loved seeing bubbles in the tub. Once the water got to a level that was enough for them to sit but not be harmful, it was ready for me to get them in. Also, the water was sufficient for them not to splash onto the floor since it would give me more work I didn't want.

I grabbed Sammy, the most daring child, and undressed her to place in the tub first since I couldn't trust this child. After placing Sammy in the tub and securing her safety, I turned around to grab Joey, a calm, tamed one. I undressed Joey and put him in the tub. I kneeled on the floor and was about to bathe them when the doorbell rang. Thinking it was my mother, I got up from my knees and ran to the door.

I expected to see my mother standing at the front door, but no one was there. Instead, I only saw an unknown white car parked in the space in front of our building dedicated to the fire hydrant. I looked around, and about to close the door, I saw the car window lower with a familiar voice.

Noel was so damn lazy that he couldn't wait less than five minutes for me to open the door when he was already in the car. Of course, he could have just walked into our apartment, but no, the king of the castle had to ring the doorbell for me to stop what I was doing to attend to him.

"What do you want?"

Noel's response wasn't clear enough for me to hear.

"What?" I couldn't hear him initially and walked down a few steps to understand what he was saying.

"Where is Mom?" he asked for the second time.

"She is at Tio's house," I responded quickly with the kids on my mind because I knew they were in the bathtub.

"Let me get back inside because I have the kids in the tub."

I raced up a couple of steps, closed the front door, and ran to the bathroom to ensure they were okay. They were both fine, just playing with some toys.

I kneeled back down and poured the soap onto the washcloth to start rubbing their little bodies. I would usually sing songs to make the process easier, but I just wanted to rush and get them to bed. I wanted to be asleep by the time my mother arrived home. After unplugging the tub, Joey, Sammy, and I watched the water lower in amazement. I grabbed Sammy to stand her up and wrapped the towel around her body. I dry her off and start putting on her clothes. I heard someone at the front door, so I paused and listened to the sound of keys. I dressed her, assuming my brother finally used his keys to enter the apartment. I finished dressing Sammy and placed her back in the crib.

Walking out of the bedroom, I looked to my left and saw my mother walking toward me. She had a facial expression I didn't want to see. Just by her facial expressions and walk, I knew it would be a rough night for us all. I proceeded to walk into her room to place the first child down. I turned around to walk back to the bathroom and grab the second child. I see my mother standing in the hallway with her head turned toward the bathroom.

"So, you were outside while Joey and Sammy were in the bathtub?" she asked with a stern, monotoned voice.

"Well, yeah, your son came ringing the doorbell asking for you," I replied while walking past her to grab the second child.

I bent down to grab Joey and placed him on the toilet so he could be tall enough for me to dress. I felt my body shaking and needed to tell myself to continue doing what I was doing.

Stay calm. I remind myself.

Finally, I finished dressing Joey. I grabbed him and placed him on the side of my hip. My mother was still standing there waiting for me to finish.

As I walked past my mother, she shoved the side of my head. "You were outside being a little hoe while your sisters were in the bathtub," she shouted.

I didn't react to her shoving my face, and I continued walking past her to place Joey in the crib. Then, I turned around to head toward the kitchen to grab their milk bottles so they could lie down. As I stepped the first foot out of my mother's bedroom, she repeated, "You were outside being a hoe while your siblings were in the bathtub."

I turned toward her. "Mom, it was Noel in that car." I usually would say "your son" when referencing him, but this time I needed to say his name so it would somehow click in her brain. If I didn't know the car he was in, she surely won't either.

"I saw you were talking to whoever was in that white car outside," she replied as if not caring that I told her who it was. She continued, "Then you saw me coming, and you ran up the stairs."

I looked at her, confused because I didn't see her. I ran up the stairs because I knew I had the kids in the bathtub. "Mom, it was your son asking where you were, and I spoke to him for five seconds," I replied, still trying to keep my cool, but at this point, our voices started to elevate.

"I won't leave you here for you to act like a whore. You were supposed to be taking care of the kids," she continued her accusations.

I knew that no matter what I stated, she wouldn't believe anything. "Mom, I need to get the kids their bottles," I demanded so she could leave me alone.

"Oh, now you are worried about them," she questioned. I didn't reach the refrigerator when the first hit across my face happened. The second hit across my face occurred when she asked me, "Why were you outside being a whore?" She continued hitting me while I blocked my face. Finally, I yelled back at her, saying it was Noel, her son.

I'm trying to block her hits from my face, and she is trying her hardest to destroy me. I had to try everything to get away from her. Finally, the only possible way for me to walk was backward, which led me into her room.

"Mom, it was me outside." I hear my brother's voice confirming what I already told her.

I'm still walking backward when I hear my sister screaming. They had a front row seat to my abuse. My brother is behind my mother, still yelling that he was, in fact, the person in the car.

"You think I'm stupid, you little bitch," she yelled while I felt the next blow to the face.

I felt like I was outside of myself. Struggling to keep myself up and present, I felt the next hit. Each side of my body was getting a turn of blows.

My mother kept yelling words I couldn't make out. The more she screamed, the stronger she became.

She continued over and over again for what felt like a good five minutes. Feeling a sensory overload, I freaked out and pushed my mother back. Everything went silent, and all I saw was a blur. I couldn't make anything out of where I was, but I knew I was somewhere in her room. The worst thing I could have done was push her back. The sudden rage that entered the woman standing before me came from the devil. I tripped and fell back onto the floor in the cramped space between her bed and the wall. I fell back so hard that I hit my head against the wall. I couldn't see anything but felt this woman's hands gripping my ears. Her nails scrapped my scalp, and she dug them deep into the back of my ears. She grabbed my ears so tight and started banging my head against the wall.

All I could do was think at this point that I would die. My mother would break my neck and kill me. At sixteen years old, I would die in front of my siblings. I heard my brother again, but I couldn't see what was happening or where he was. I felt my strength starting to deplete. "Mom." I hear a voice far away. "Mom, Mom." I heard it again, and it gave me the strength to raise my knees toward my chest, and I gave it all I had in me and kicked her.

I felt a hand grab my arm and pull me off the floor. I stumbled out of my mother's room through the kitchen and into my room. She followed me into my room and grabbed my stereo system, which was huge, and threw it toward me. My brother was still trying to calm her down and leave me alone. I didn't say anything else to her. I sat on my bed and just cried. She proceeded to make my siblings their bottles so they could fall asleep.

I sat there looking her way but ensuring she didn't see me staring at her. I needed to be aware of her every move. I didn't understand why this woman hated me so much. I started questioning everything.

Why was I her punching bag?
Why did she even give birth to me?

Why am I even alive if God knew I would go through this with this woman?
Why me?
Why did she believe I was a whore?
Why did she want to kill me?

These questions continued running through my head. I did what I knew how to do best. I slowly drifted off into a space where I remembered great moments.

My mother wasn't a horrible person but a person who did awful things. My mother being terrible wasn't the case all the time. My mother was great at dominoes. Puerto Rican dominoes consist of a lot of counting. Counting numbers to make sure you know the hand your opponents will play. She taught me the game, and she taught me well.

The numbers are from zero to six. The double-six is the most substantial number to throw down on the table. Four players, set of two teams, to play at a time, with each person having a hand of seven dominoes. Your teammate sat across from you, and you could not communicate. The game's objective was to be the last person with no dominoes, and whichever team got to five hundred points won. Traditionally, men play this game and pass it down to the family males. My mother consistently defied that objective. She wanted me to be just as good or even better at the game than the men in our family.

"It isn't just about the numbers but how good you can read your opponents," she said.

"How can I tell?" I asked very curiously.

"Look at their body movements. My mother explained that if they look uncomfortable, they don't have a good hand," she explained.

So curious to learn more, I stood over her looking at her dominoes. Then, I paid close attention to the dominoes on the table to guess the other players' hands.

"Which one do you think I should play?" my mother asked.

A little hesitant to answer because I was afraid to make a mistake, but she encouraged me to trust my instincts.

Once I knew my mother had fallen asleep, I started throwing my clean clothes into a laundry bag to prepare myself to leave her home. I knew I could not continue living with her because one day, I would die at the hands of a woman who gave me life.

CHAPTER 4

THE NEXT DAY

I opened my eyes with barely any sleep and got up quickly to prepare for school. I dressed and walked into the bathroom as quietly as possible. Turning on the light in the bathroom drew my attention to the mirror. Staring at myself for a few seconds, I analyzed the damage. My face never looked so horrifying. Then, after a deep breath, I washed my face and brushed my teeth.

Every morning, my cousin, Chewy, would ring the doorbell for us to walk to school together. However, it was not a bright idea for him to ring the doorbell today. The last thing I wanted was my mother to notice I was leaving. The damage she had already done was enough.

There was bruising all over my left eye, and the sclera was completely red. I didn't see any white in my eye. Even though I could barely see out of my eye, I could still use it. Also, I felt the back of my ears burn to the touch. I shed some tears while the questions came racing back into my head.

Why me?
Why does she hate me?
What did I do for her to do this to me?

My body was sore, so the faster I tried to move, the more I felt the pain. The pain spread to parts of my body that I had no recollection of being hit. Finally, I walked out of the apartment, raised my hood over my head, and waited for Chewy outside. The distance I saw him walking gave me the knowledge of when to turn around once he came closer. I didn't let him see my face because I wanted to avoid him asking any questions.

As we walked to school, I kept quiet.

"What's wrong?" Chewy asked.

I started to explain to him. Finally, I lowered my hoodie, and his face was in shock.

"I didn't know your mother would do that to you," he stated in disbelief.

I raised my hood over my head as I looked down. Because I've always protected my mom, many family members didn't know what my mom could do. I never wanted anyone to see her as an evil person. I prefer people to believe I was the problem before believing she was a physically or mentally abusive parent.

Due to my lack of interest in attending classes, I walked into a staff member's office at my high school. Over the years, I developed a cordial relationship with Janina, an attendance officer at the school. Although I knew she was trustworthy, I was still apprehensive. I walked into her office and sat on a chair across from her. As I sat down, I hid my face beneath my hoodie. I felt her staring at me, so I got up from the chair and closed her office door. She realized something had happened.

"What's wrong?" she asked.

I couldn't even respond before I started crying. Finally, I took my hoodie off and faced Janina. Her eyes opened so broadly, and with shock all written on her face, she asked me, "Who did that to you?" I wanted to lie and tell her a group of girls had jumped me. But I knew if I lied, she would pressure me to tell her what girls, where, and when and try to get all the information.

So, I explained to Janina what exactly had happened, and she didn't respond.

Since Janina was a staff member in a public school, she had an obligation to make a call. She had an obligation to make a call to DCFS. DCFS stands for Department of Children and Family Services. The organization's mission is to protect children from abusive and neglectful homes and increase their families' capacity to care for them safely.

Janina had other students walking in and out of her office, but she didn't want me to go to my classes. So instead, she had me sit outside her office. I didn't mind sitting on the floor if no one else saw my face. Janina requested classwork from all my teachers to keep me occupied, which was good for me. It would help my mind stay off what had happened the night before.

"Here's what I've received from your classes." She passed me a stack of papers.

"Okay."

I sat on the floor and kept my face on the papers. I didn't pay attention to anyone passing by me. I just focused on completing my classwork, so I stayed caught up.

Throughout childhood, my mother repeatedly told me, "You will never amount to anything." Those words drove me crazy. I refused to let her be right about me. I cried, but I couldn't allow anyone to see me. I was able to get through it by taking deep breaths and focusing.

"You can't go back home," Janina said to me.

I looked up at her with a sense of humiliation. I felt my face turn so red because I didn't know exactly where I would go. Who is going to want me?

"Do you have family members you can call and stay with until DCFS reaches out to you?" Janina questioned.

My mind went blank, and I started feeling the nerves run throughout my body. I started questioning myself once again.

Was this a good idea?

Should I have said anything to her?

If my mother finds me, she is going to kill me.

A sudden sense of fear came over me that left me feeling stuck. I couldn't move or talk. I'm officially lost. I didn't know where life was about to lead me.

"Daisy," I said. I knew my mother wouldn't contact her if she decided to look for me. Moreover, Daisy would not give in to my mother if she did. If needed, Daisy would defend me from her or anyone who came after me.

The next day, the case manager visited me at Daisy's apartment.

"Hello, Janell, my name is Sherry." She explained to me who she was and the process. "Do you have any questions?"

The first process: "Walk me through what happened the night of the event. Be as specific as possible."

I proceeded to explain everything to Sherry. However, she sometimes interrupted me to ask the approximate times the events occurred.

The second process: "I will need you to remove your clothing." I was so hesitant and wanted to cry. I removed my clothing with such embarrassment, and it wasn't only because of the bruises on my body but because I didn't want to show her how fat I was under all the layers of clothing.

She held a clipboard and a sheet of paper showing the outline of a human body. During the examination, she circled on the report where she saw marks. She quietly studied my face, back, breasts, stomach, legs, and arms but forgot my head. She didn't even think of checking behind my ears, but I did ask her to look. She saw the evidence of my mother's nails. When she first touched my left ear, I felt the pain and made a slight noise. She flinched, and I waited for her to give me any instructions.

"I'm sorry," she said. "Please pull your ear forward so I can see what is behind them. I don't want to hurt you."

I did as she asked.

I stood quietly, waiting for her to tell me to dress. Instead, she looked at me and said my mother told her she defended herself against my hits.

The third process: an explanation of what to expect next. The caseworker also explained to me the version my mother provided. Upon hearing the accusation mentioned to Sherry, I became so enraged that I disassociated.

"Look at the numbers on the building," my mother said.

I looked up while we walked, and I saw the numbers changing.

"Okay," I said.

"In the direction that we are going, the numbers are going up, which means we are walking from east to west," she continued.

My mother was teaching me how to tell which way I was heading by looking at the addresses of apartment buildings we were passing.

"If you are ever lost, you need to be able to explain to someone where you are at, Janell, so pay attention."

Despite my understanding of the north, west, east, and south, I still needed clarification. What child at seven would honestly know all of this? However, I paid attention.

"Mom, how do I know I'm not going south to north?"

She giggled when I asked the question. Her response was quick. "Look at the sun. The sun will tell you everything."

"Janell," the caseworker said.

By the caseworker saying my name, I snapped out of my disconnect. But I continued listening to the accusations.

I suspect she lied because she didn't want me to leave home so she wouldn't lose her free babysitter. There was no way I was ever going back to her house. Then I thought that *if she created the story of me talking to a boy, she might believe I tried hitting her.* So, I told the caseworker the entire story, and I did admit I kicked her off me, but it was merely to save my life.

Eventually, Sherry believed me and provided Daisy with temporary custody of me. This temporary custody provided me with a place to stay until I turned eighteen. After that, however, I had to manage on my own.

CHAPTER 5

MY JOURNEY

"Nell!" Sammy said.

I heard the tiny voice, and I quickly looked to my left. There I saw Sammy, my sister. A chunky curious face is staring straight up at me with her index finger in her mouth, biting her little nail. Joey and Sammy stood before my mother as she spoke to one of her friends. My two greatest loves are waiting for me to embrace them. How could I not? I was hesitant to walk over to my siblings, but with my heart aching, I still wandered over anyway.

For about a year, I didn't speak to my mother. Instead, we acted like strangers when we encountered each other on the streets, on public transportation, or in family homes. Not speaking to one another affected not only me but my siblings as well. She wasn't interested in speaking with me, and we shared mutual feelings until I was about to graduate from high school.

"Could you let my mother know I'm inviting her to my graduation?" I asked Teresa.

Teresa was Noel's Godmother and an excellent friend of my mother's. My mother was in a dilemma and living with Teresa at the time. I was walking east on Augusta Boulevard, and I so happened to bump into them. It was a perfect chance to invite her so I could rub it in her face. After all, she would always say I was never going to graduate.

Our relationship remained cordial after she watched me walk across the stage. After that, however, our mother-daughter bond was not pleasant. I don't recall my mother saying "I love you" or hugging me because she couldn't show her vulnerability. The same was true of me. I did not know how to express mine either. Yet, despite it, my heart has always been there for my mother.

With my first goal accomplished, I needed to decide my next step. Living with Daisy afforded me the freedom to be myself, but I learned a lesson early on about working and becoming independent.

One morning, I woke up and walked into the bathroom. I tried turning on the bathroom light to start prepping for the day. As I looked around, I thought, "That's weird." The lights weren't working, so it was dark. Leaving the bathroom, I walked to the kitchen and tried those lights. Nope, they didn't turn on either. So, I called Daisy at work.

"Hello," Daisy said.

"The lights are not working," I explained.

"I know," she responded.

I paused and didn't know what to ask next.

She explained that I wasn't doing anything with my life and that she needed to teach me a lesson.

Daisy did not place any restrictions on me while I lived with her. It was okay for me to do whatever I wanted, even at a young age, as long as I kept my promises to her and maintained my goals. When DCFS placed me with Daisy, I was still working at the movie theater. I needed to keep that job since I needed it to purchase my items. Then I got depressed, and I fell into a rut. For many reasons, I left the movie theater job and wasn't doing anything with myself.

"If you don't have money to pay a bill, then you won't have light," she said.

As a result, I now knew I couldn't rely on anyone, but she taught me that lesson and used me as an example to my other cousins.

Daisy always said, "If anyone could do it, it would be you. I'm surely not allowing you to be lazy."

Ironically, having no lights in the apartment lit a lightbulb in my brain. I started working at an attorney's office where Daisy also worked. Finally, at eighteen, I landed a job working for a well-known bank in Chicago.

Between those jobs, I considered joining the air force. A career in the air force could have provided me with so many benefits and kept me out of Daisy's way. I spoke with several recruiters, and they helped me set up the test. In preparation for the following examination, I stayed at a hotel near Chicago O'Hare airport the night before.

I was nervous because it wasn't like I had studied for this test. I also had to wake up at 5:00 a.m., and I'm not a morning person. So, I jumped on the bus to take me to the testing center early on the day of testing. I walked in and saw some men in uniform screaming in some recruit's face, and I freaked out.

After living with my mother for so many years, I had PTSD and was not ready to repeat that experience. How could I now, after staying away from my mother's house for years, sign up voluntarily for her to yell at me? At that moment, I realized that no amount of monetary incentive would convince me to sign up.

I looked at the exam papers and sat down at the desk. Since it was early, I was hungry and traumatized by what I had just witnessed. I could not read these questions. So instead, I filled each circle with eeny, meeny, miny, and moe rhymes. I did pace myself, so they didn't notice I was flying through those questions.

When I saw other people finish, I got up and handed them my paperwork. They provided me with the score, but to no surprise, I could have done better. I acted like the score shocked me but I felt relief. They explained how I could study and come back and retake it. I told them, "Yes, I will." I lied. That answer was a big *no*.

Initially, I worked as a receptionist at the bank, which was easy. Over the years, I have worked in various departments and locations. I was able to experience many firsts in my life while employed at this financial institution. I experienced my first vehicle purchase, my first apartment, my first bank account, my first degree, and many other firsts with them.

A coworker, Linda, sold me my first car. Linda helped me obtain the loan from the bank, but they were only willing to loan me a portion of the amount. Unfortunately, I did not have the remaining funds. However, she offered me a deal. She suggested I babysit her kids on weekends and whenever she needed a sitter during the week.

It was a great deal. Despite not having a license, I said yes and got my very first car. Yes, I lied to the bank and the insurance company about having a license. Since the technology wasn't as advanced as now, it was easier to do so back then.

During my time there, I also acquired my first apartment. I did not have much in my apartment, but I had a bed and a few pots and pans. I struggled to keep it up, but I am no stranger to working. I know how to eat a mayo sandwich if that is what it takes to accomplish my goals.

As I viewed the goals and aspirations of many others, I knew I could not stay stagnant either. My goal was to achieve what they had, even if it meant working double time. Despite my mother's protestation, I was eager to prove her wrong. As some of my old coworkers came from families with money, I did not have that luxury. But I did not allow that to hold me back. Instead, it pushed me to say I got everything on my own.

Furthermore, being around such professionals made me realize I was not brilliant. In both my appearance and my speech, I differed from them. In half of the cases, I didn't even understand what they were saying, and I was so afraid to ask that I just stuck to numbers.

Damn, my mother was right. I wasn't brilliant after all. Those words bothered me to the core, and I knew I needed to expand my knowledge. I wanted to enroll in school to get my bachelor's degree, but I faced a challenge. Since I was under twenty-four, I had to apply with my parents for financial aid. So, regarding school purposes, it didn't matter whether I lived with my parents or not.

As soon as I learned the requirements, I assumed my parent's answer.

Mom said, "You don't live with me, so you are no longer my responsibility."

My stepmother Sandra told me, "We will only help you if you move to Michigan and attend schools here."

Again, I was facing a challenge in life because they weren't willing to help. I don't know why I even bothered asking them.

I enrolled in classes and paid for them in cash. It was difficult, but I did and later learned that the bank would reimburse me if I took business courses. Unfortunately, the classes I enrolled in were not eligible for reimbursement during my first enrollment since they were not business classes. Initially, I had no idea what I was doing or wanted to major in, but I just knew I wanted to learn.

I tried applying for financial assistance every year without my parents, but I kept getting rejection letters which meant I had to continue paying my classes in cash. Finally, when I applied to DeVry University and told them about my situation at the age of twenty-three, they allowed me to apply for financial aid on my own.

Although this was not an Ivy League school or even close to other universities in reputation, they allowed me to attend school while working full-time. However, my parents refused to help me out all these years, which pushed me so far back that I didn't want to wait any longer to get a degree. I knew obtaining a degree would help me get a job in a bank that didn't involve retail work.

I worked full time at the bank and attended school four days a week. I was doing homework at home on days I wasn't working or in class. Back then, there were no online classes, so I was tired almost every day, but I was determined to accomplish this goal.

I was barely getting by on a small budget during my college years. After living on credit cards for many years, I claimed bankruptcy once but kept this a secret. Although it was a fresh start, it was embarrassing. Moreover, it was embarrassing to admit I failed just as my mother predicted. Even so, I worked harder and didn't allow this misfortune to stop me.

CHAPTER 6

THE BEGINNING

When I die, I don't want anyone crying.

A few years later, I received a phone call from my cousin while I was at work. "Janell, have you spoken to Tio Eddie?" My cousin would pick up my uncle to take him grocery shopping for the food and items needed to prepare the graduation dinner for Tio Eddie's son, who was graduating that weekend.

"No, the last time I saw him was Sunday when I dropped him off from our trip to Wisconsin," I replied.

"I'm calling his phone, and I hear it is ringing, but he isn't answering the door," she said.

"Did you try pounding on the door?" I asked.

"I've even asked the employees from the building," she stated with worry.

"Call Daisy to see if she can get into his apartment." Daisy is my aunt, who is Tio Eddie's sister.

"I'm going to call her, and then I'll call you back," Lilly stated.

I continued dealing with the client I had at my desk. At this time, I was working for a bank. All my clients knew me very well, so it didn't bother them that I answered the phone. Usually, I won't answer personal calls, but this weekend was momentous, so I excused myself.

My phone rang again, and I saw it was Lilly once again. "Daisy just got here, and we are trying to get into his apartment." At that moment, all I heard were screams. I couldn't make out who was screaming, but I heard words I never wanted to hear.

"Janell, he is dead."

I hung up the phone and told everyone I had to go. I ran out of the bank so fast and didn't care who was sitting at my desk. Once I got outside, I looked around to find my car. I was trying to remember where I had parked. Thoughts played in my head during my last moments with my uncle.

Before this day, we spontaneously got into my new car and drove to Wisconsin for the day. We were having a few drinks and dancing when his boot started shifting. They amputated a percentage of his foot. Since we were dancing, the boot began to twist and was no longer in the correct alignment. I bent down to fix it for him, and he told me how proud of me he was and to never forget that he loved me so much.

Still bent down on the ground, I looked up at him and told him, "I know, and I love you as well."

While dropping him off in front of his apartment building, he got out of the car, bent down, and looked at me. He said, "I love you, and be careful home." Those were the last words I heard come out of his mouth before he took his own life.

I parked and took the elevator up to his apartment on the fourth floor. I tried to go into his apartment, but my aunt didn't let me. I needed to see him, and she didn't allow me to.

"I don't want you to see him like this, Janell." My aunt wanted me to remember him by the last day I saw him. Five days after his death, someone discovered his body. My uncle suffered from depression. We all knew his struggles, and he attempted to take his life in the past, but he was still with us. Sadly, he blended all his prescription medications and used them to end his life. He could have done this a day after I dropped him off. To this day, I question myself was this day a way of saying goodbye?

Waiting in that hallway, I recalled Tio Eddie sitting at my cousin's funeral almost a year earlier. He was hurting from her death. Although she wasn't his daughter, we spent much time together. Several years prior to her death, Rajeeni and I had an apartment together not too far from Tio Eddie's apartment. He would sometimes just come over and have drinks and chat with us. One night we all pulled some seats in front of our front window to watch cars pass and talk about everything. Drinks in our system, and after many laughs, the conversation started to get very serious.

I remembered one of our last conversations we had together in that apartment.

"When I die, I don't want anyone crying," Tio Eddie said. I froze and just looked in his direction. He continued saying, "I want everyone to party. Have a good time with music and dancing."

"Yes!" Rajeeni responded. "We are going to party our asses off." I looked at her in disbelief that she was even entertaining this conversation.

She saw my facial expression, looked straight at me, and said, "What? We will all die, and when I die, I don't want any hypocrites at my funeral."

I got up from my chair and walked toward the kitchen. I paused and turned around. "I don't want to talk about death with either of you right now."

So now, here we are a year after Rajeeni took her own life my Tio Eddie took his as well. Her method of taking her own life was different, but she still took her own life. I never really mourned her loss. Instead, I threw myself into working and school to keep my mind occupied. Her mother and my mother are sisters, so we were raised very close. We were more like sisters. Although she was two years younger, she always made it seem like she was older than me. She was a protector all the time. For several months leading up to her death, she and I didn't speak. Our not speaking was just time and distance. Life happens, and it gets in the way of our relationships.

After this event, I knew I had to take time off from school. I needed to sit and mourn the loss of two important people. I needed time to be myself and not fall into depression. Depression took the life of my family members, and I refused for depression to take mine.

With no classes to worry about, I started to hang out with my friend Jezreelita. For short, we called her Jessie. Jessie lives in the Humboldt Park area of Chicago, where I grew up and went to high school. She and I met in high school when I was about thirteen. After graduating from high school, we didn't see much of each other until we started working together at the bank. So now I could spend more time with her outside of work.

A woman always enjoys receiving an invitation to an event that requires dressing up. Unfortunately, I had little time to prepare to attend the graduation of the little brother of my best friend, Jose, whom we called Papo. I wore a tight white shirt, black pants, and small heels. Something I threw together to look presentable, but I didn't realize how loose these pants fit until I started walking up the stairs. With every step I took, the pants slowly lowered past my hips. Finally, I stopped on the steps, pulled them up, and held onto them so they wouldn't keep falling. I felt a little embarrassed because those following behind me were Papo's friends, who were all guys.

"If that's your way of flirting, all you have to do is say it," said one of the guys in the group. I ignored him and kept walking up the stairs to make it to our seats on time. I don't know who the voice was today, but we were all running behind, so I didn't care to entertain the situation.

We entered the arena and looked for seats that would be enough space for about fifteen people. Papo invited his friends and family so we could celebrate since graduating high school was a significant struggle for him, so we all went to be substantial support. Sitting to the right of me was my best friend, Jezreelita.

A few seats down, a guy kept looking at me and smiling. He would hide his face when I would look, and everyone started laughing. I felt the interest coming from his energy, but it embarrassed me because I knew he was much younger than me. He was very handsome and tall, with light skin with long braids. There was some chatter from the other friends, but I ignored everyone. We laughed it off, and with perfect timing, the graduation started.

Some time passed, and I didn't see him for a while. I was so busy going to school full time and working full time that I didn't have time to entertain anyone. Let alone a young man when I was already in my twenties.

One night I went to Jessie's house, where she lived with her parents. Her neighborhood was bustling. It was a very rough area, but everyone from there knew each other, and it was like one giant family. Although we lived in the same area of Chicago we were from different blocks which housed different types of gangs. Those who lived on my block usually wouldn't hand out on the block Jessie lived on. I had never lived on Fairfield Ave, so I was a new face to many. They knew I was her friend, so no one ever bothered me, but many were interested in me. I never cared to talk to anyone there because they were all involved in the streets, which wasn't anything that caught my interest.

Standing in front of her house, I noticed the guy from Papo's graduation was present. I'm naturally a quiet person that stands back and observes everyone. It was a hot summer night. He was walking toward her house, and he stopped and grabbed the water hose on the corner of her house lying on the grass. He proceeds to try and wet his hair. He has such long thick curly hair that the water was bouncing off instead of his hair absorbing. I started laughing because it took ten minutes for the water to soak his hair. He drops the water hose and flips his hair back. All you see is his hair flipping back and all the water falling back with his hair's motion. I couldn't remember his name, so I had to ask.

He walked into Jessie's front yard, where we all were standing. He walks right past to stand on the step of the front door. With the jokes he was telling, he made everyone laugh, including me. The laughs were a relief at the moment. The only person that knew my emotions was Jessie, so she knew I was enjoying the moment. I looked straight at him and enjoyed every moment he made jokes. He started to act like he was a flamboyant gay man. But he did it in such a way of comfort and not in a disrespectful way at all. My Tio Eddie was a gay man who struggled for years. Although he was open for many years before his death, it wasn't easy.

So, it played out very well when Carlos acted out his joke. He just laughed, and I put my head down so he wouldn't see me laugh. I felt a spark, but I told myself it couldn't be true. I must be delusional.

Every year Chicago holds a festival for Puerto Rican heritage. It is usually a week of carnival in the park, followed by a parade on the Saturday before Father's Day.

That Saturday, Jessie and I discussed going over early to her house because they started closing the streets, and it would be difficult for me to get in. I got to her home at about 11 a.m. and parked on the side of her house. It was initially an alley that the city closed off, so there was space. I was the first car there, so I had a clear view of my car just in case anything happened.

Right next to where I parked was an empty parking lot that the guys from the neighborhood would use as parking for this event. Fencing surrounded the parking lot, so they would illegally pop the lock and open it so cars could park. When I pulled in, I noticed that Carlos had climbed the fence so he could place the Puerto Rican flag on the top. I see him jump off and drop to the ground when I get out of the car. Minding my own business and trying to pull my things out of the car, I didn't care much. But, when I look up again, I see he is holding his right hand with his left. He walks to the front of Jessie's house and drops to his knees.

I see Jessie's Mom, Lucy, come out to see what is happening as I walk toward them. She runs inside the house, and I walk past him while looking down at his hand. I didn't see anything, but she ran out with a first aid kit. I walk into the house and place my things on the sofa. I walk back out, and I hear them saying he is going to need stitches.

Papo runs down the block to where Carlos's dad lives so he can let him know what is going on. His dad walks over, and they need a ride to the hospital. Jessie volunteers to take them to the emergency room. I stood in her house getting ready while she gave them a ride. She dropped them off, and a few hours later, she received a call that Carlos was ready. She asked that I go with her, so she didn't go alone, so I agreed.

"How are you feeling?" Jessie asked him once Carlos and his dad got into the car.

"I'm fine. I just got stitches. I was about to pass out because I didn't like the sight of blood," Carlos explained. I chuckled a little bit but didn't say anything to him.

"Do you want to be my nurse?" he asked me. I was embarrassed because he said it in front of his father.

"Sure," I responded, but I didn't even turn around. Everyone just laughed.

Hours passed, and more people showed up for the festivities. Finally, Carlos's family showed up, but they were on the opposite side of the empty lot. I see them looking at me. I walked toward my car to put my bag in so I wouldn't forget it later. I look up and see his family walking toward me, smiling. They stop in front of my car. His sister, Yana, was holding her son, Yaniel, who was six months at the time.

Before adequately introducing me to his family, he proclaimed, "She is going to be your aunt."

"Don't say that, Carlos." I laughed, and I felt my face turn red. I didn't know him, and he had already stated something crazy in front of his family. They all laughed, and I spoke to them for a little while before heading back to the front of Jessie's house.

Carlos only stuck around a short time after because the Puerto Rican fest usually had harmful activities with local gangs. His family requested that he take them to their home in the suburbs. He didn't fight and left with them, intriguing me even more. The respect he had for his parents was significant. He lived with his father part time in the city and part time with his mother and stepfather in the suburbs. The relationship and love he had for all of them were major. He knew they would worry about him, so he left with them.

The next day was Father's Day. They were going to be celebrating Father's Day at Jessie's house. I didn't think I would see him, so I didn't count on it. I was about to leave to take some food to my mother, and I saw him on the block.

"Are you leaving?" he asked.

"I'll be back. I'm going to take this food to my mom," I responded. We looked at each other and just smiled.

"You want to take a ride?" he said.

"Sure."

He gets into my car, and we drive off. The look we got from everyone on the block was one of shock. My phone rang, and it was Jessie. "Why is Carlos with you?" I laughed because that news got back to her so fast. I drove off just seconds ago.

"He is coming with me to drop this food off to my mom," I explained.

She sounded like she was in significant disbelief, but I was enjoying the moment. I wasn't putting too much thought into any of it.

Carlos did go upstairs with me and met my mother. Meeting my mother wasn't a big deal for me at all. Our relationship wasn't great by any means. I left her home at sixteen and didn't speak to her for over a year after I left. So now, anything I do, I don't care for her opinion. As I explain more of my story, you will understand why I didn't care.

I don't think Carlos knew this introduction didn't mean anything to me.

We left my mother's apartment to get back to the block before they started shutting down the streets once again. Entering Fairfield, we looked at each other and smiled. It was a connection we both went for and shared our first kiss. I remember telling myself to enjoy this summer. Enjoy this moment. It is just for this summer.

CHAPTER 7

SUMMER NEVER ENDED

"Carlos, let's go to Mexico," I said excitedly.

Yes, Carlos. The same Carlos that was supposed to last just for the summer is still in my life a year later. But this time, I'm planning on taking a trip with him. I purchased a timeshare in Rivera Maya, Mexico, a few months prior. I had no clue what I was doing, but I wanted to do something different. Creating memories that last forever was something I take pride in over any tangible gifts. Anyone who knows me knows I'm not a big gift giver.

As a couple, we wanted to create memories that would last a lifetime. I didn't realize how much fear I would feel when I decided to step out of my comfort zone to experience new things when planning the trip. The nerves in my body were trembling, making it impossible for me to sit still. I had a lot of negative scenarios going through my head, as if the trip would be disastrous.

I had never traveled to Mexico, so I didn't know what to expect. It wasn't my first time leaving the country but traveling internationally and using my passport. I had never flown anywhere that required a passport. My family and I had traveled to Canada before, but I only had to carry my ID, and Border Patrol never checked my ID. We were flying to Mexico, so I had to show my passport. It would be my first stamp. Excitement and fear of perhaps never returning home caused nerves.

On the plane, they passed out some forms to fill out with the intention of our visit. I read it, and for some reason, my brain didn't comprehend anything on the paper. Carlos grabbed my form and just started filling everything out. One for him and the other for me. I can't recall if we had to sign it, but he did pass the form back to me, so I could hold it until we landed. Carlos explained the process, so I could try and calm down. He did say we were going to have to go through Border Patrol. They will ask questions but stay calm. They look for suspicious people and can decide to check you if they feel or see something funny randomly.

Carlos's father is from Honduras, so he has visited his family since he was young. His mother's family is from Puerto Rico, but he had never visited the island. So, in his mind, everything was okay and normal because it was something he had grown accustomed to seeing since he was a young boy.

As we exited the plane, I made sure Carlos was behind me the entire time. He smiled at me and assured me everything would be okay. We walked up to the Border Patrol. He looked at our passports and looked at us. He asked us a few questions. Everything was good, and he let us pass.

Our next step was to find our luggage and then ride to the resort. Having located our vehicle, we boarded it and handed our bags over to the driver. As I looked around, I noticed Carlos was so calm. Being in a foreign country left him unfazed. Neither of us knew where we were heading, and he didn't care. There was nothing but a smile on his face. He was at peace. It gave me a sense of ease I had never felt before, and I knew we would have a memorable time. The military checkpoints were visible as we drove out of the airport. Carlos laughed because he saw my facial expression. They were in a pickup truck with weapons on display. I'm assuming they were rifles that they were carrying. There must have been about six men on the back of the pickup truck, with two men as driver and passenger.

"Do you not see this in Puerto Rico?" Carlos asked me.

"No," I responded very quickly. I thought to myself, why would I see this in Puerto Rico?

"Well, you see this all over Honduras," Carlos started explaining.

I didn't want to stay fixated on the military checkpoints, so I just tried to look around and see what I would like in Mexico. I wanted to know if there was any difference between the United States and Mexico. There was mostly grass, trees, and no development. We continued heading to our destination, which was about a forty-five-minute drive from the airport.

We pull into this massive, developed grounds. Pulling into the property, we had to stop, and the front gate held a guard. We both look around in shock at the view in front of us. I thought to myself that I did well. My spontaneous purchase was a great deal. From the pictures, it looked very upscale but not to the level we currently were viewing.

Walking into the lobby, we both looked around and immediately felt out of place. We didn't have the money to stay here, but we had to play it off as we did. Then, finally, the hotel staff came up to us.

"How can we help you?"

I responded very quickly, "We have reservations."

"Okay, what is the name of the time shareholder?"

At the time, we were not married, so I responded with my maiden name and gave her my passport.

"Oh, you're so young to be an owner."

As Carlos and I looked at each other, we just laughed. The situation was utterly unknown to us, and they were right. We were both young. I was twenty-five, and Carlos was eighteen. Despite me being twenty-five, I just looked like I was a teenager. So, we weren't surprised to get her reaction.

We received our room key and directions on getting there, but we still needed help. The resort was huge, and we were eager to look around, but we needed to free ourselves from all our belongings. Finally, we walked into our room and were astonished by its beauty.

Carlos and I both come from modest beginnings. Many people from our neighborhood rarely leave the country, let alone the state. Our families did not expose us to life's finer things. Being at this resort was a shock for us.

The hotel room was more of a small apartment. As soon as we walked in, it was the kitchen area with an eat-in dining room and living room with two sofas and a TV. Off the living room was the main bedroom entrance leading us to a bathroom. The toilet had its own space in the bathroom.

We walked through every room excitedly, and Carlos smiled with excitement, kissing me and throwing himself on the king-size bed.

"Are you planning to take a nap, or are we planning to wander and explore?" I asked Carlos.

I was excited to check everything out, but he reminded me that we were there for seven days, so we had plenty of time to explore. So, I let him nap while I sat on the sofa and let it all soak in.

The next day, we headed to the pool, where there was a happy hour. Carlos wasn't a drinker in the States because he wasn't of age, but he said he would have a few drinks with me. I wasn't a big drinker, but I wanted a good time, so we decided to enjoy the specials. It was another way for us to stretch our dollars. We found a spot to lie by the pool, and he asked what I wanted to drink. He walked to the bar and got us our drinks. I got a mudslide, and he got a strong drink.

We sipped our drinks and let the sun hit our pale skin. Even though I burned under the sun, I thought I might look dark. At the time, I was a fool for thinking that. Onto our second drink, and Carlos was all smiles. He kept saying the drink was so delicious, and he didn't understand why it took him so long to start drinking. I did have to remind him once that he wasn't old enough to have alcohol. As we continued to drink, we laughed at our ages.

"Carlos, my stomach hurts," I said.

"What's wrong?" he asked.

"I don't know."

He laughed and mentioned that the name of my drink was mudslide for a reason. I opened my eyes wide and told him we had to go. He grabbed our stuff so fast, and we hauled ass to make it back to the room. He made fun of me the whole way there, but I held my laugh because I didn't want to have an accident.

"Stop, Carlos," I requested but with a smile on my face.

He was having too much fun seeing me feeling sick. I knew he wouldn't let me live this down at all. The smile on his face was from ear to ear.

"Memories," he blurted out, which made me laugh.

We made it back to the room without any accidents on the way. He checked on me to make sure I was okay before he decided to take his daily nap.

Later that day, we went to a local store to buy food to cook in the room instead of eating out all day. The resort staff suggested Walmart when he asked where we could shop. Taxis would take us there, and then they would wait for us to take us back. At that time, I had no experience converting dollars into local currency, so I handed all the cash over to Carlos.

At the resort, security wrote down our names, room numbers, and the taxi's license plate. Carlos knew how to handle himself in a foreign land, so I felt safer around him. To make the ride more enjoyable, he started asking the driver all kinds of questions. We returned to the resort safely after shopping.

The next few days, we planned out different excursions through the resort. We didn't want to sit around at the pool and drink. We wanted to experience Mexico. If it were up to Carlos, we would have just left the resort with one of the locals and experienced Mexico as one of them.

He made friends with a resort employee. He couldn't be so public with their newfound friendship, but every time he saw us, he would get excited and yell out Chicago. He did mention that they had specific rules regarding relationships with guests. Of course, we vibe more with the employees than the guests, but we understood.

The first excursion we embarked on was horseback riding. The host mentioned that they matched us with a horse based on our personality. They assigned me a horse that was all white with a black tail. She was calm, sweet, and beautiful. They gave Carlos a horse who was a jerk.

He kept biting all the other horses in the ass. He didn't stay still and kept moving all over the place. We laughed so hard because they sure did pick our horses correctly. The best part of the horseback ride was jumping into the water with the horse.

Carlos opted out of swimming with the horse because he didn't feel safe doing so but stood back to take pictures of me while I experienced a great memory. I was scared going in because they explained how the horse would start making funny noises. We also had to ride in without a saddle and hold onto the horsehair, which made me feel bad.

I stayed in for about ten minutes, and I came back out. I saw Carlos from afar, just paying attention to me. Making sure nothing went wrong but also taking in my smile. We looked at each other and just knew we were both so happy. He witnessed something I'd never done, and that made him so happy.

A few days passed, and we decided to do another excursion. This one, we wanted to dress up and experience the nightlife in Mexico. We purchased a package that would take us to three different clubs in one night with unlimited drinks. They also picked us up and dropped us off at our resort. Carlos heard "all you can drink," and he was in without questions. The night was going great. We met several people on vacation from the States or Canada. I'm the shy one in the relationship, and Carlos is outgoing. So, when I say we met, I mean he met, and I followed along with a smile. Just how our dynamic worked.

We were at the second nightclub, and Carlos left me talking to some girls we met on the excursion. He felt I was safe and comfortable with them. All hammered at this point, they all wanted to touch my breasts. "Yes, God blessed me with my breasts," I kept repeating to them.

They couldn't believe it and wanted to keep touching me. Finally, Carlos came back, and I explained what was going on, and all he could do was laugh. "You are a lucky man to have all of that," they mentioned to him. He laughed but wasn't paying much attention to what they were saying. I saw he kept looking toward the front of the club.

Toward the front of the club, you see the DJ and the dance floor. Behind the DJ was a massive projector that displayed different pictures. They had us in a VIP area toward the back of the club, which I enjoyed because I wasn't in the crowd. However, he saw I was busy with this drunk woman, and Carlos was trying everything possible to get my attention to look toward the projector. I was trying to understand why he wanted me to see pictures of what was happening in the club if I could see it live for myself.

When I looked, I saw Carlos had professed his love for me onto the projector. The big words he used in such large print for everyone to see surprised me. I can't remember the words he used since it was so long ago, but I know it was professing his love for me. I didn't react fast enough to take a picture because I stood there and let it all sink in. I live in the moment. It was a wonderful moment because he did it in front of everyone without care. I felt so much love for him. I couldn't believe he did that for me. I turned to him and just hugged and kissed him. It made my night.

We were so excited about his actions that neither of us paid attention to anything else. We returned to the van we came in and sat down, ready to go back to the resort and sleep. Carlos was already falling asleep with his big head on my shoulder. I couldn't say anything to him because he had just made such a grand gesture. I was not going to tell him to move his head. We noticed we were almost the last people in the van. After learning we got in the wrong van, we asked how long it would take us to get to our destination.

Carlos asked, "What do you mean by the wrong van?"

We didn't hear an announcement informing us that we would return to the resort in another van. So having been in the van for about an hour, we were now in Tulum. It's so easy for Carlos to fall asleep anywhere, so he falls asleep again. On the ride back, I tried to stay awake out of fear of someone kidnapping me. I held on to Carlos's shirt the entire way back to the resort as he had his head on my lap.

I felt my eyelids getting so heavy that I had to shut them for a bit, but my mind wasn't thinking they would take us somewhere else. I opened my eyes so quickly but felt the warmth of Carlos under my hand. I looked at him, sleeping so peacefully, and it calmed me down. I placed my hand's palm on his chest and felt a sudden sense of peace. I laid my head back and prayed to God that everything would be all right.

I closed my eyes again, pictured the projector with Carlos's lovely words, and I dozed off for a bit.

CHAPTER 8

IN SICKNESS AND IN HEALTH

I felt the van stop. As soon as I opened my eyes, I sat up quickly. As I looked around, I noticed we had made it to the resort. Thankfully, we didn't get kidnapped.

"We're here, baby," I said. As soon as Carlos lifted his head off my lap, he sat up. He glanced around before looking at me and smiling. I followed behind him as he got out of the van. After he exited the van, he turned around and held his hand to assist me. We walked quietly from the parking lot to our room, holding hands. Looking at him as he walked toward our room, his actions filled me with a sense of security and admiration. I never wanted to lose this feeling.

We were indeed the best of friends, doing almost everything together. I never got sick of him. There was never a fight between us. Over the years, even though we had disagreements, we learned more about how to deal with one another as the years progressed. Several rules guided our relationship.

Rules:

1. Never argue with each other in public. We have each other's backs and correct each other in the privacy of our homes.
2. Never allow yourself to sleep mad.
3. Never ignore each other.
4. Always answer the phone to one another.
5. Always respect one another.
6. Never call each other by our names, not even jokingly.
7. Never curse at each other, no matter how angry we are.
8. Never get involved in any dispute with the in-laws. We handle our own blood families.
9. Always be honest.

Throughout the years, I continued to attend classes to obtain my bachelor's degree in business administration, graduating in 2007. Together, we worked hard and discussed our future and would achieve what we wanted out of life. Our first attempt to move to Florida failed because I received another opportunity in the bank that would benefit me. After discussing it, we decided to stay in Illinois.

Something in me tends to be an overachiever because I tell myself I'm not good enough. I have a stable job and boyfriend, but I still feel empty. *Your accomplishments so far need improvement. You obtained that bachelor's degree, but now what will you do?*

I gave myself every reason why I should return to school. So here I go, after my first master's degree in accounting and financial management.

It is now two years later. I was in awe when I opened our doors and looked down the stairs. There was a tea candle on every step leading up to our apartment door. A feeling of anticipation filled me as I smiled. As I walked, my heart beat faster and faster. I paused for a moment as I stepped down to the final step. A wall blocked my view of the apartment door, so I glanced over and saw him on his knees. Although I knew he would do it, I still needed to learn exactly how he would do it.

"Love, will you marry me?" Carlos asked.

"Yes!" I said with excitement.

I knew he was shopping for rings on the day he received them. Out of excitement, he couldn't wait to pop the question and placed the ring on my finger. Four years into our relationship, we are now engaged.

Several months later, Carlos got hurt. Two surgeries later, we decided to have a small wedding since our income had changed, and we didn't want to continue waiting to get married. One of the major decisions was because being just a fiancée doesn't give me any rights to speak with his attorneys, doctors, or employers regarding his current situation.

Carlos started getting depressed, and it was challenging for him to give me any decisions regarding our wedding.

"Carlos, I need your opinion," I said.

He was sitting on the sofa in our living room. I felt his disinterest.

"Carlos," I repeated his name.

He walked to our room and looked at me with no facial expression.

"Do you still want to get married?" I asked.

"Yes, but I don't care about any details," he responded.

I felt sad because it wasn't like him not to be involved. He always wanted to provide his input in anything that we did.

Unfortunately, his surgeries didn't deliver the results we thought he would receive. He was still in a lot of pain but trying hard to be optimistic. A few days later, I got home from work, and he was sleeping. I looked into our freezer to see a bottle of Patron. There were about a couple of shots left in the bottle. I poured it out and placed it back into the freezer. That's when I realized Carlos was battling depression.

We discussed his current feelings and situation to develop a game plan. I wanted to proceed with a wedding only if he felt up to doing it. He refused for us to cancel it. I did worry that he was still recovering from his surgeries. He asked his doctors for release to travel. As long as he wore his brace, he was okay. Several weeks later was our wedding, only six months after his surgeries.

We flew out to Puerto Rico.

"I, Carlos, take you, Janell, to be my wife, and I do promise and covenant, before God and these witnesses, to be your loving and faithful husband in plenty and in want, in joy and in sorrow, in sickness and in health, as long as we both shall live."

"I, Janell, take you, Carlos, to be my husband, and I do promise and covenant, before God and these witnesses, to be your loving and faithful wife in plenty and in want, in joy and in sorrow, in sickness and in health, as long as we both shall live."

Just like that, we are now married.

Several months later, Chicago was hit by its third-largest snowstorm ever. Carlos had to dig himself out of our apartment to clear our vehicles because we lived on the ground floor. It was important to him that I could get to work without public transportation. Because he was still recovering, I didn't want him to deal with the snow, but he didn't like someone telling him what to do or staying still, either.

We are the opposite when it comes to weather. I was not too fond of the cold, so I opted to stay inside, but Carlos loves to feel the cold. So, while he worked outside in the snow, I stood in our apartment, cooking him a delicious meal. I cooked a massive steak and served it with mashed potatoes and corn on the cob. It's impossible to go wrong with corn on the cob since he loves it.

"Love, I fell," Carlos said.

"Are you okay?" I asked.

He was still recovering from his surgeries. They placed titanium rods in his spine, so the cold didn't do well with him. I worried but couldn't show him because he would brush it off.

"Baby, are you hungry?" I asked to get his mind off his fall.

"What did you cook?" he asked.

I explained what I cooked, and his whole face lit up. He was excited that I surprised him.

Several weeks later, I gave my two weeks' notice at work. Carlos and I decided that the cold, ice, and snow didn't benefit him. Plus, we felt being in a warm state would help him with his depression, recovery, and us. So, I gave them my two weeks with no job lined up in Florida, but I had faith. My husband's health came first.

We got all the approvals we needed from his workers' compensation to move and find doctors in Florida. We packed and made all the plans. We got into our vehicles on May 31, 2011, and headed to Florida. After settling in, we were enjoying our life, trying to learn everything we could about this new city. We were having fun discovering Orlando. Our favorite theme park was SeaWorld. We both love animals so much. Unfortunately, Carlos couldn't get on the rides because of his back, so I didn't either.

I decided to wait for employment to help Carlos with everything, including his mind. I knew he was sad because his injury limited his ability to do many things. However, I wanted to do as much as possible to keep his mind busy and off workers' compensation issues.

Several months later, I experienced something I would never imagine happening.

"Carlos, stop!" Vanessa, his cousin, yelled.

Carlos stood right in front of her, threw a punch, and hit the wall behind her. Rage consumed him. Vanessa didn't show him any fear. After he threw the punch, he walked away from her. He was yelling down the street. "Motherfucker."

"Janell, he needs help," Vanessa said.

As I sat on the steps, I felt lost. I didn't feel anything, not even fear. It was time to decide what I should do or where I should take Carlos.

I called my sister, Ely. Ely isn't biologically related to me, but she is a longtime friend I call a sister to cut down any explanations to anyone. "I don't know what is happening to Carlos, but he needs help," I said. She showed up fast to help me take him to a local mental institution that would help him with his depression.

Ely had been living in Orlando for several years before our arrival. She knew the area more than we did. She dove us to the facility, where Carlos had to sign himself in.

"Are you sure you want to do this?" I asked Carlos.

"Yes, I never want to see the look on your face again," he said.

This face he speaks of is the face of helplessness. Until this day, I have always known what to do. I'm naturally a problem solver, but once I heard him screaming like a mad person, I knew I couldn't tackle this issue. I witnessed my husband remove all his belongings and walk into the facility. I was curious to know how long he would be there. I walked to the car and sat there. I cried my eyes out.

I haven't slept without my husband in years. How am I going to sleep? I felt desperate because I didn't know how he was doing. I lay in bed crying because I wanted him home. Then, a day later, Carlos called.

"According to the doctors, I should not be taking my medications at the same time," Carlos explained.

"What do you mean?" I asked.

He continued explaining that the medications he was on for depression and painkillers counteracted one another. Consequently, his body reacted aggressively due to this counteraction.

"I'm sorry for putting you through that, my love," he said. "Are you coming to see me?"

I didn't hesitate to visit him. I had to be there at a specific time, and they only allowed an hour. I went every day until they released him. It destroyed me to leave him there, and I cried every time I walked out of the building. Once he was out, he listened to the doctors on how to take his medications, which was short lived.

CHAPTER 9

OVERDOSE

My head turned to the sound of pills hitting the plastic of a bottle. The noise each capsule makes when they hit each other and the plastic bottle tends to spike my anxiety. I stared straight at Carlos to see what he was doing in the kitchen with those pills in his hand.

"What are you doing?" I asked him.

"I'm counting the pills in the bottle," he replied.

"Why? You just got the bottle," I asked with a face of confusion. He picked up the prescription of Xanax from the drugstore a few seconds ago, so for him to walk in and count them was a bit suspicious. His body language was a bit off as well. He was nervous and jumpy at the same time. I was trying to figure out what was wrong with him.

"How many did you take?" I asked him. He looked at me with hesitation to respond, but he knew he needed to give me a response.

In the past, I would have to count his pills every so often to ensure he wasn't taking more medications than he should have been taking. For a while, I stopped it because it was a tiring responsibility. He wasn't my child. I needed to ask him this time because he wasn't acting like the same Carlos as every other day. I got up from the sofa to walk over to the kitchen, but before I even reached the countertop, he rushed to put all the pills in the container. I stood at the end of the kitchen counter and stared straight into his eyes. He already knew what I was thinking, and I had to either argue with him or leave the situation alone.

Upset, I turned around and walked toward the room without saying another word to him. Carlos noticed my facial expression. "What?" he shouted out loud, to which I continued walking into my room. I needed to ignore him and calm myself down. I grabbed my pajamas to get ready for bed. I thought about him overdosing on his pills once again. He has done it in the past, and I felt it would happen again this time. I closed my eyes and stood under the shower, trying to have a positive mind. After taking a shower, I lay down, staring at the ceiling and praying that I don't wake up to anything outrageous. After a few seconds, lights out.

Everything was dark, but I could hear the sound of the TV. I slightly opened my eyes while extending my arm to feel the left side of our bed. I didn't feel Carlos next to me. I opened my eyes and looked to the left to confirm he wasn't lying beside me. I looked at my room door to see if it was open or closed. I see the light from the kitchen and TV. While half asleep, I forced myself to get up from the bed. My heart started beating faster with every step closer to the living room a little faster. Once I reached Carlos, my heart felt like it wanted to come out of my chest. I looked down at him, afraid to even touch him. I stood over him for five minutes, but it could have been just a few seconds. Once I got the courage to touch him, I heard the sound of his snoring. It was loud, but I had never been so relieved to hear that annoying grumbling that sounded like birds chirping.

On my way to work the following day, I could only think of Carlos. I just had his image in my brain for the entire thirty-minute ride down the highway. Then, finally, I just pictured his whole body lying on the reclining sofa. His mouth was open, snoring, his hand on his chest, and his legs spread apart with his socks on. I prayed he was okay. I didn't want to wake him up, but at least I knew he was alive when I left. I parked my car and sat just for a few seconds, looking at the office building.

"God, please give me the strength to conquer this day without any issues. Please give me the strength to pretend to be a happy person. Give me the strength to be able to work." I sat in my car to say these words out loud. The anxiety I felt in the pit of my stomach was so intense that I wanted to place my hands over my eyes and cry. I couldn't do that because then I would fall apart. I needed to keep it all together for me and also my household. I needed this job, so I couldn't allow anything to affect me. Finally, I managed to get out of my car and walked toward the building. Every step of the way, I just spoke positive words to myself. I reassured myself that everything would be okay.

I had an appointment later on in the afternoon to go out to audit a business. I watched the time to ensure I left with enough time not to be late. I was counting down the minutes to get out of the office. I grabbed my phone to look at the time my phone started vibrating in my hand. I waited for the name to show up on the screen, and it was Carlos.

"Hello," I answered.

"Hello." I hear a voice on the other line respond. It wasn't Carlos's voice at all. I looked at my phone to ensure I did see my husband's name come up on the screen. I placed the phone back on my ear.

"Hello." I started once again with a nervous shake in my voice.

"Is this Carlos's wife?" the man on the other line asked me.

It took me a few seconds to respond, and he wasn't sure if I had hung up. "Hello?" he asks.

"Yes, this is his wife. To whom am I speaking?" I asked.

"This is Willie from the barbershop," he responded.

Since he was still sleeping, I did not expect him to make it to his haircut that morning. So, I was surprised his barber was calling me and was nervous.

"How can I help you?" I asked him.

"Well, I don't know what Carlos took, but I found him on our bathroom floor. It looked like he tried to vomit in the toilet and didn't make it," he started explaining to me. I sat and listened to him, but all I could think was, damn it. I have an audit to conduct, and I can't get out of this for Carlos' shenanigans. So, I started cursing Carlos in my head. I was so upset and just responded with an attitude.

"Did you call the ambulance?" I asked. I heard a gasp of air from Willie's end. He didn't expect me to ask that question. I should have asked if he was okay, but if he had called me calmly, I figured he was still alive.

"No, I did not call the ambulance because I don't know what he has on him, and I don't want him to get into trouble," he continued, saying he felt it would be better for me to handle the situation myself.

With frustration, I told him, "I'm sorry, but I'm at work, and I can't leave my job for this. A few days prior, I had to leave work early because Carlos wasn't feeling well." I didn't want to have to request to leave early once again.

"Let me call my sister to see if she can go over there, and I'll call you back."

I hung up the phone and quickly dialed Ely's number. Hoping she answered because she usually likes ignoring her calls. Surprisingly, she answered the phone so happily. She sounded like she was with someone in her car. I asked her if she was busy because this was important.

"No, Ma, what's up?" she asked.

"Carlos's barber called me to say he vomited and passed out on the bathroom floor." I paused because I heard her say, "What the fuck!" Because I couldn't leave work, I asked if she could help me go over there to see what was happening. As I explained to her what was happening, I grabbed my things and headed out to conduct this audit. "Okay, I'm on my way, and I'll call you once I get there," she said.

I quickly called Carlos's phone back, hoping that someone would answer. Once Willie answered, I explained that my sister was on the way to the barbershop, and once she got there, we would figure out what to do with him. Ely called me once she arrived. "He is still passed out but is breathing," she stated with worry.

"Take a picture of him and send it to me." I know how Carlos looks when he is in terrible shape or sleeping. When the picture arrived on my phone, I anxiously opened the message. They placed him in their employee break room sitting up. He had his head leaned back against the wall with his mouth open. His lips were so pale you could tell he wasn't good. Ely was still on the line waiting for me to give her instructions.

"Ely, his lips are white. Please call the ambulance." While I'm giving her the instructions, you can hear Willie explaining how he found him.

"She is telling me to call the ambulance," she explains to Willie.

"I don't know why they didn't call the ambulance in the first place," I said angrily.

"Okay, I will call the ambulance and let you know what happens," she responded.

"All right, I have to go into this audit. I will try to pay attention to the phone, but if I don't answer, I'll call you back," I explained.

I had to walk into the place of business, acting like nothing was happening in my world. I had to forget what was happening to do my job correctly. I sat at a desk and looked at everything this business owner gave me. I couldn't focus. I feel my phone vibrating, and typically they don't allow us to answer our phones, but in this case, I just had to, given the circumstances.

"The ambulance is here, and they won't take him because he has weapons on him," she explained.

"Please take everything he has and take it to my apartment," I requested.

I stayed on the phone with her while she started emptying his pockets. In amazement, she started listing out what he had. He had a gun, an extra magazine, more bullets, and a knife.

"What did he think? Did he think he was going to war?" she asked jokingly.

I didn't respond to what she just questioned since I honestly didn't know how to answer. She told me which hospital they would take Carlos to and that she would meet them there.

"Before you go to the hospital, please go to my apartment to drop everything off and count the pills." I wanted to know what he took so we knew what to tell them at the hospital.

As soon as she called me from my apartment, I debated whether I should continue the audit. I couldn't focus on my job because I was so angry with Carlos. After finding the Xanax bottle, Ely read the label. There were thirty pills for this prescription in the bottle, but only nineteen remained. The number of pills left in the bottle caused my brain to calculate how many pills he had taken.

"Ely, he took eleven pills of Xanax in less than nine hours," I explained to her with my voice so upset.

"Ma, that's a lot of pills in a short time," she responded. He took a pill every hour. I questioned how he was still alive.

"I don't know if he took anything else, but I know he just got the prescription filled last night," I stated. I continued to tell her how I saw him last night, very anxious, and just asked her to go to the hospital to see what was happening.

At this point, I knew I needed to end the audit. I found any excuse to leave the business owner's store to get home. Wrapping up the paperwork, I explained to the business owner the following steps to this audit and that I would have to continue reviewing his paperwork later. He was a bit confused, but I didn't care to explain my situation at home. I got into my car, and Ely called once again.

"The nurse said I need to keep Carlos awake so his oxygen doesn't drop. If it drops, they will have to pump his stomach," Ely explained to me.

"Don't stay with him. Let them pump his stomach," I demanded.

"They said if they do that, he will be in a lot of pain," she responded

"So, he needs to learn his lesson." I didn't care if he felt pain. I wanted him to feel pain. All the pain he could discern so he could stop doing this.

"Leave Ely," I demanded once again. Finally, she did leave the hospital. I headed home, debating whether I was going home first or straight to the hospital. I needed to calm down, so I decided to go straight home.

While on the highway home, Carlos calls me. "They won't release me until I have a ride home," he quickly explains.

"Okay," I responded. I honestly didn't care to rush.

"Where are you? Are you coming to get me?" he asked.

"I'll pick you up, but you will have to wait," I said sternly.

I did call Ely and told her not to answer his call because he was looking for a ride. I wanted him to wait until I got there so he could suffer more. I went home and showered. I needed to stand in the shower and let the tears come from my eyes. I needed to let it all out before I got to him. He always hated seeing me cry. At this moment, he wouldn't care how I felt. I knew he would still be high and upset with me for showing emotions.

I braced myself to pick him up and played every scenario in my head of the encounter with my husband. Due to this being a habitual action for him, I knew he would fight with me. I'm the one he takes his anger out on. I walk into the emergency asking for Carlos Peña. They gave me a pass and pointed toward the direction of his room. Walking down the long hallway, I felt I would never reach him. I felt every step I took toward his room the further away it seemed. I was getting very nervous at this point, even to see him. Finally, I entered his room and stood there looking straight at him. He looked up at me and laughed.

Seeing and hearing his laughter pissed me off.

How could he think all this was so funny?
Does he not know I was tired of this?
If he wants to take his life, why continue saving him?
Why keep putting me through this shit?
Lord, take him.

At that second, I felt so bad that I even thought that way. A sudden urge of rage rushed through my body. I needed to tell myself to calm down.

"This isn't funny," I said to him with an attitude. I walked over to the chair that was across from his bed.

"What took you so long?" he asked but not in a clear voice.

"I went home to take a shower," I responded.

Carlos looked at me with shock on his face. It was a *how could you* type of look. Then, we started arguing, and a nurse walked in. She looked at me, confused as to why we were discussing.

Great, another person who thinks I'm just a bitch. She proceeded to tell me what they didn't want to do, but at this point, they had already stabilized his oxygen levels. When she said they didn't want to pump him because it would leave him in pain, I reiterated what I told Ely. "You should have pumped him so he could learn his lesson." She turned her head so quickly toward me as if she couldn't believe my response.

I continued with my attitude and stated, "This isn't his first time doing this." I just wanted to be precise.

"Well, he needs plenty of rest so his pills can wear out of his body."

I looked at her with a blank stare. I wanted to respond, "Rest was the last thing I would allow him to do." I knew if I said that to her, she would think I wasn't compassionate.

I waited for his release to do the exact opposite. If he were to put me through this suffering again, I would also make him suffer.

Throughout this story, I kept thinking about Kim Kardashian and Kanye West. Despite Kim's support, Kanye was unable to control his behavior. As a result, I empathized with her and understood what she was going through. Kim wrote a lengthy explanation on her Instagram story, which she deleted, but thankfully, you can still find it on the internet.

> As many of you know, Kanye has [bipolar] disorder. Anyone who has this or has a loved one in their life who does knows how incredibly complicated and painful it is to understand.

> Those that understand mental illness or even compulsive behavior know that the family is powerless unless the member is a minor. People who are unaware or far removed from this experience can be judgmental and not understand that the individual themselves have to engage in the

process of getting help no matter how hard family and friends try (Toone 2020).

I don't know what Kim has gone through with Kanye, but what I do know is that I can sympathize with her. So let me ask you a question. Have you ever tried calming down a child throwing a tantrum in the middle of a store while others were looking?

CHAPTER 10

DISCHARGE

Trying to calm a screaming child, you can't help but feel a moment of embarrassment. All your blood is rushing toward your face since you feel others passing judgment. You are doing your best but can't help from blushing and sweating. I felt the same way. Even worse, I have to walk out of the hospital room with discharge papers in my hand. I knew all the nurses would look at me with such shame. I looked down at those papers to see his name written across the top. A sudden rage entered my body, and I quickly turned around to see if Carlos was following me or still in the room. I see him about six feet behind me, strolling, smiling, and joking with the nurses. I felt my whole body shake because I just wanted to hit him.

I looked at the nurse walking beside him, and she stated, "Oh, he is in good spirits."

I knew he was acting at that moment. He wasn't well, but he knew what to do so they won't keep him. So, I waited until he got closer to me to continue walking.

I kept telling myself, *show compassion, Janell, show some fucking compassion.*

As we walked out of the hospital, I told him what we would do. We were not going home for him to sleep. We needed to run some errands. I didn't have to run errands at all, but I wanted him to stay awake and feel everything the nurses didn't want him to handle. If he was making me feel exhausted, overwhelmed, mad, and hateful, I wanted him to feel the pain. Yes, I know you may question why I feel such a way toward my husband. Honestly, I just wanted to cry when I sat in my car. I looked over at him, and he had no care in the world. I started to think about why he would do this again. If he wanted to take his life, he just needed to do it and stop playing Russian roulette with his life. What happened to him affected me, but he didn't understand.

As I drove toward my sister's house, my mind didn't stop playing with every past scenario. Why didn't I act with compassion as I have in the past? Could it have been because he knew how to win over the hospital staff? Was it because he flirted with my friends in the past because he was under the influence? Was it because he loved the pills more than he loved me? Was it because he knew I experienced several suicides in my family and wouldn't leave his side? Was I enabling this behavior? What did I need to change so he wouldn't do this again? How did things go wrong?

Then a sudden feeling of guilt came over me. Janell, how can you not care if he dies? He could have died. Then another rage of anger came over me because I felt guilty. Then I thought about how he got himself to the barbershop. I remembered he drove himself. Not only did he put himself in danger, but he also put other people's lives in danger. I felt disappointed because it wasn't the first time he had driven under the influence. He didn't learn from his experience. I looked over at him, and I saw he was falling asleep.

I hit his arm so he could wake up. "I told you I wasn't going to let you sleep." He woke up and looked at me like I had disturbed his entire life.

We walked into my sister's house, and she quickly started asking him questions. She knew the game plan of keeping him awake until I felt like taking him home. She is good at asking him all the questions I wouldn't ask or maybe I didn't care to ask.

"How many pills did you take?" she asked.

"I don't remember," he replied.

"I counted eleven pills missing from the Xanax bottle. Did you take anything else?"

"I didn't take that many," he replied.

"Carlos, you got a brand-new bottle last night, and eleven are missing. If you didn't take them, then who did?" I asked him with an attitude.

"I only remember taking about three of them. The first one didn't seem to affect me, so I took the others," Carlos said.

"You must have taken them every hour on the hour because eleven pills were gone in less than nine hours," Ely said.

"Do you want me to count your pills again?" I asked.

He looked at me with a confused look on his face. At this point, I wasn't angry but more emotional. My heart was aching, but I was holding it all back. Finally, I felt my eyes starting to get watery, so I walked away from him so he could continue speaking to Ely about the situation.

I sat in the living room and looked straight at them as they continued their conversation.

"And you drove that way," Ely said, prompting Carlos to inquire where his vehicle was.

"I drove it to your apartment."

I couldn't help but remember the incident while I was on vacation. A few years before this incident, I left for Puerto Rico for Ely's grandfather's eightieth birthday party. I needed to get away from Carlos for a while. I needed a break from babysitting my husband. He thought I was going out there to be with a guy.

Yes, he created a story in his head about how I would be out there with some guy Ely and her husband were friends with at the time. I had no clue who this person was and had never met him. I didn't even know or even care that guy was going. He said he put two and two together and wasn't stupid. I didn't argue with him. I just left him to believe what he wanted to think. I needed time away from him, and this was a perfect escape from my reality. The birthday party would be a big celebration, and I wanted to enjoy it. I wanted to be in a tropical paradise, drink, and dance without worrying about anyone ruining my night.

I feel my phone vibrating on the day of the birthday party. I saw it was Carlos and it was six in the morning.

"Hello," I answered softly since my friend Milly was sleeping.

"I'm in the hospital," I heard come out of Carlos's mouth. I woke up fast, got off the bed, and walked to the living room to sit on the sofa.

"What happened, Carlos?" I asked with desperation.

"I got into a car accident last night," he explained.

"Carlos, were you high?"

His voice was as if he was still high and trying to lie to me. "No, I wasn't high."

"You're still high," I said.

"No, I'm not, and they tested me," he replied.

"Carlos, you can fool everyone else, but I can tell you're high. I'm sure they didn't test you for your meds," I said angrily.

"I need a ride home," he said.

He knew I was in Puerto Rico and couldn't pick him up. So, I told him I would call a friend to see if he could get him. Once we hung up, I called our friend Gilbert. I wasn't sure if he would pick up the phone, but surprisingly he did.

I explained the situation and asked if he could pick Carlos up from the hospital. He told me, "Janell, I was with him last night." Those words prompted me to ask him questions to confirm that I wasn't crazy.

"Was Carlos on his medication when you were with him?" I asked.

"Yes!" he confirmed.

"Carlos wasn't happy that you were in Puerto Rico and feels you were with someone," Gilbert said. "I didn't believe his accusations and told him he needed to calm down."

"Was he drinking?" I asked.

"Yes," he replied.

"Well, after you left my house, Carlos got into a car accident and totaled out his work vehicle," I said.

Carlos decided to satisfy his craving for a McFlurry from McDonald's, which could have cost his own life and another person's life. He rear-ended someone on the side of the road, damaging her car, injuring her, and totaling the pickup truck.

I reached out to his mother and spoke to one of his sisters that day. I felt judged by both because I wasn't planning on flying back home to attend to him. After all, they didn't believe me when I said he was driving high. His sister lived in Tampa, so she went up to tend to Carlos, and I was okay with that, but for them to pass judgment on me without knowing the entire story was frustrating. So, from many miles away and over the Atlantic Ocean, Carlos still managed to fuck up my day. Maybe this is another reason why I'm so cold with him.

Feeling sadness come over me, I just wanted to bust out crying. I looked at Carlos and said, "Let's go home." Not so that he could rest but because I needed to rest. All these situations took a toll on me, and I needed to lie down and sleep. The only way I would get to relax was to pretend the rest was for him. I had to act like I still had compassion.

CHAPTER 11

BAKER ACT

Mental health is a frequent ride on the emotional roller coaster. One day you may feel everything is under control, and the next day everything is about to go nuts. Believe me when I say this emotional ride doesn't happen just to the caregivers but to the professionals trying to handle their patients. Let me explain to you why I make such a strong claim. Carlos knew how to manipulate any situation, especially if it would get him out of trouble with his doctors.

"You're heading the wrong way," I yelled at Carlos over the phone. I had no clue where he thought he was going, but Carlos said he was heading to his psychologist's office. He was on Route 50 heading east toward his psychiatrist's office when he should have been on Semoran Road heading north. It was about a five-mile difference when I called him.

"Turn around," I demanded because I didn't want him to miss his appointment. Today would be very significant for the psychologist to see him in these conditions. I'm sure you are wondering why he was heading the wrong way. I needed him to get to this appointment so badly. Carlos drove to his appointment at a very high speed. I can't even tell you what pills he had taken.

However, he was notorious for taking many medications and drinking alcohol, so I wouldn't put it past him that he did such a thing early in the morning. But, no, I couldn't drive him because I was at work. So, I stayed on the phone until he told me he had reached his destination. It was the day Dr. Horn, his psychologist, would see how Carlos behaved, and I eagerly awaited his phone call.

Not even five minutes into his appointment, my phone rang. "Janell, it's Dr. Horn."

I knew who it was, but I allowed him to speak. "Yes?"

"Carlos came for his appointment but is in no condition to drive," he explained.

"I knew he wasn't," I replied.

Dr. Horn sounded surprised when I told him I knew, but I waited for him to ask me more questions. "You let him drive like that?" Dr. Horn asked with a little bit of judgment coming from his voice.

"How else can you see what Carlos does when you aren't around?" I sighed. "How you see him now is how he acts daily, and no one believes me. He knows how to play everyone, and I'm tired."

"He needs help, Janell," I heard from his end, which had me a bit confused. *You are his psychologist, so why can't you help him?*

I said, "Yes, I know, so what are the next steps?"

Being polite to all the doctors, nurses, and family members who did not deal with him daily was getting old. It makes sense to me that Carlos has a charming personality, and his humor makes the party come alive. You can't be mad at him for too long because he speaks to you so that you can't hold it against him.

Carlos knew how to manipulate any situation to his advantage. Any time he had an appointment for a doctor's visit, he was on his most conscientious behavior. They have repeatedly heard him say that he takes his medication responsibly, but he is depressed and managing as well as he can. He left after they talked for an hour.

After that, he was free to do whatever he wanted, including taking his medication. When I say popping his meds, I mean he knew precisely how many he could pop and how much he could drink without killing himself. He played with his life daily.

"I think you should take him to the hospital," Dr. Horn suggested.

After thinking about it for a moment, I said, "No."

There was a long pause on both ends of the phone. Dr. Horn was shocked, and I was frustrated.

"Honestly, Dr. Horn, I already knew what he would do if I showed up. All he would do is fight with me there and in the hospital, and I don't have time for that today," I explained passionately. I didn't even want to see him at the moment.

"Well, I knew if I called the ambulance, he wouldn't make it easy for anyone," Dr. Horn said.

Really? Is what I thought to myself. Let's not make anyone else's life difficult but mine. Is that what I just heard? In disbelief at what he had just suggested, I couldn't speak because I was so upset. When I get upset, I'm the type of person who starts to cry.

The cause of my tears isn't from hurting right now but frustration over being unable to solve the situation. I had to compose myself for a moment before I cursed him out. It probably took too long for me to finish my second sentence, and he continued explaining the situation. It wasn't what I wanted to hear, so I tuned it out, but Dr. Horn said, "We have a better chance of cooperating if you are with him."

With a deep sigh, I tell him, "Okay, but if he starts fighting with me, then you have to handle it because I don't want to deal with him."

He agreed.

It took me thirty minutes to drive to Dr. Horn's office from where I was working. On my drive there, I was contemplating every scenario possible:

1. I wondered how he would treat me in front of Dr. Horn.
2. I thought about how upset he would be if I arranged for all this to happen.
3. I was thinking about how tired I was and that he needed help.

I pulled into the parking lot and sat for a few minutes. The situation I was about to enter required preparation on my part. I put a suit of armor on, so anything he would do or say, I didn't take it personally. It all sucked. It was impossible to live this way. *Get out of the car Janell. Today is the day he will get help.* With this wishful thinking, I pushed myself out of my car and walked into the doctor's office. There was no one else there but Carlos and Dr. Horn. I waited for

Dr. Horn to lead me back to where Carlos was sitting.

Inquiring eyes asked me, "What are you doing?"

"Dr. Horn called me to come."

"I don't need you here," he quickly stated aggressively. Again, I looked to Dr. Horn because I already knew where this was leading.

"I called her here so she can take you to the hospital," Dr. Horn explained to Carlos.

As if he were looking at an enemy, Carlos asked, "How can the hospital help?"

"You are not well, Carlos, and we—" the doctor started to explain, and Carlos quickly interrupted him.

"You did this," Carlos furiously exclaims.

In response, I said, "You did this to yourself." At this point, I wanted him to argue with me so Dr. Horn could see the honest Carlos.

"I'm not going anywhere with you," he said.

"Believe me. I don't want to be here now." I grinned at him, which I know pissed him off even more. Suddenly, his facial expression changed. His body language changed. His entire demeanor shifted. The only thing I could do was stand by the door and watch him. There is no way for me to know what he can do when he is in that state of mind. Although he has never hit me, I cannot underestimate what he can do to me or anyone around us when he is so high and experiencing a manic episode.

"I'm not going anywhere. I was talking to Dr. Horn, and you showed up," he started to mumble out his mouth but never got up off the chair.

Before any argument escalated, Dr. Horn intervened and explained his options to Carlos.

1. He cooperates and goes with me to the hospital.
2. We call the ambulance, and they will sedate him and still go to the hospital.

After providing Carlos with his options, he said, "We can do it the right way or the difficult way."

The entire time Carlos was looking at me like he hated me. I looked straight at him because he could never intimidate me, but I also was waiting for his response with the hope he would say he would instead go in the ambulance. Nope. He opted for me, his wife, to take him.

"I'm not arguing with you in the car. We are going straight to the hospital, and I don't want to discuss anything else." That is what I demanded from Carlos for me to agree to drive him.

I received direct instructions from Dr. Horn on what to do and where to go. Neither of us spoke until about fifteen minutes into our car ride. As I approached a gas station, Carlos requested I pull into it so he could buy cigarettes. I pulled into the parking lot to avoid an argument, hoping he wouldn't attempt to flee. That wasn't the case. He bought cigarettes and smoked one before getting back into the car. We didn't speak again until we got to the hospital.

Once we were inside, Carlos wasn't trying to talk to anyone. I had to explain the situation to the triage nurse, who turned around and asked him if he was suicidal.

He told them, "No." He had this great big smile on his face. He said it with his chest popped out and his voice so deep. He said it so proudly. Again, I tell you Carlos knew how to play the system.

If Carlos tells the nurses he isn't suicidal, they can't keep him against his will. Then I explained the situation again and told her that the psychologist had ordered them to call him directly. The nurses seemed to be very annoyed with me because I wasn't backing down at all. Finally, they assigned him a bed in the hallway to get me out of their hair. We sat and waited.

One nurse came over to me and started explaining, "Ma'am, we cannot Baker Act him if he is stating he isn't suicidal." Florida Baker Act is the involuntary admission to a hospital to seek help when a person is a danger to themselves. They also can Baker Act a person when showing signs of mental illness. If they knew what was going on, they would know Carlos was, in fact, suicidal and was battling mental illnesses. Not one but two mental illnesses.

At this point, I knew I needed to start name-dropping and making my phone calls. Carlos was all smiles because he was hoping they would release us. I made the phone call to Dr. Horn to explain what the nurses were saying. He told me not to worry and not to go anywhere. Then, he made his phone call to Carlos's psychiatrist Dr. Allen. I had never met or spoken with Dr. Allen, but he is well-known at Florida Hospital. I knew Carlos saw him every month to get his refills for his meds, and that was about it.

"All right, Mr. Peña, we are Baker Acting you today," one of the nurses said when she walked over to us. The sigh of relief from my entire body was so evident that Carlos looked at me with such a sad face. That was the face I didn't want to see—a hurtful face like I was doing something terrible to him. I didn't want to feel guilty for leaving him behind. I had to look down and tell myself this was for him.

"Mrs. Peña, you can stay or leave him to us. We will find him a permanent bed and have strict instructions from his psychologist and psychiatrist." I knew I needed to leave immediately, so I didn't feel guilty anymore. The Baker Act requires that a person stays for at least seventy-two hours after it takes effect. I can't get him released, and he can't do it himself, either. The Baker Act was new territory for him.

The last time he was in a mental facility, he signed himself in, so I know his emotions were different this time around. Now he had no control over the situation. Having him admitted was just one more reason to hate me even more. It would be better to have him hate me while he is alive than to be his favorite person while he is dead.

I grabbed his things and kissed him. I hated kissing his lips because he would get cottonmouth from all the meds he would take. Cottonmouth is when your saliva glands don't produce enough saliva to keep your mouth wet. It wasn't pleasant kissing him. I had to find everything in me to not cave into the look he had on his face.

His eyebrows lowered, and his eyes dropped, looking at his lap. I just prayed they would help him and he would return to normal.

I walked down the hallway until I no longer saw him when I looked back.

CHAPTER 12

INTROVERT OR NOT

"Janell, are you truly an introvert, or were you trained to be an introvert?" is a question that a life counselor once asked me.

I pondered that question for many years. If you have ever been to a counseling session, you know you can't just stick with one person. It would be helpful if you tried them out to see which will suit you best and help you with all your issues. Initially, looking for help was challenging because it wasn't something I wanted to do, but I knew I needed it. Although I had been urging Carlos to seek help, I wasn't taking my advice.

I began my journey to find the help I needed. My journey toward self-awareness has led me to consult with various experts, from life coaches and therapists to psychiatrists and even a hypnotherapist. I understand their educations differed, but they all achieved the same things, in my opinion. For example, the hypnotherapist tried to hypnotize me to heal my childhood trauma. *What the fuck is this?* I thought as I closed my eyes and let him believe he was doing something to me. My eyes were rolling behind my closed lids, thinking he needed help because I thought he was crazy. Afterward, I thanked him and never looked back. At least it was polite to avoid hurting his feelings. A people pleaser is a part of me, I guess.

In finding a life coach, I had many other trials and errors. But, finally, after all the monotonous sessions, repeated stories, and research, I found the person I needed. Kendra is a life coach. By definition, a life coach is someone who helps improve your life, feel better, and achieve your goals. She was what I needed but also what I didn't want to need.

I found Kendra very intriguing when I came across her social media page. The feeling of drowning prompted me to reach out to her. I was amazed at how quickly she took the time to call me. Working full time, starting a business, and dealing with a sick husband took its toll on me. I told her a brief synopsis of my life during that call and cried with a stranger. At this point, I knew I couldn't do it on my own.

When I first met Kendra, I worked full time for a performing arts theater. The performance art theater gave me life. As a stress reliever, I would sit in the theater and watch plays. It brought me back to my childhood, where I would daydream and escape life at home. Nothing else mattered but me pretending I was one of the main actors in the play. Then I would finish my day and have to head home.

While working for the theater, I was working on building a business. The business consisted of accounting and taxes. In my head, if I had created this business, then I wouldn't have had to answer anyone. Instead, I can work from home and be there for my husband whenever he needs me. I also needed the extra money to ensure we were financially okay since we had been struggling for some time. I couldn't depend on my husband to help, so I took on the challenge.

Our upbringing raised us to keep our business to ourselves, making explaining everything to a third person difficult for me. Therefore, I kept my problems to myself. It took the life coach a lot of effort to get everything out of me. If I were in charge, I would sit there and stare at her the entire time.

Kendra wanted to understand better who I am as a person. She initially asked me about my relationship with my mother. I immediately thought of a story about my mother's strictness toward me as a young girl. Though she felt she was doing a great job taking me to special events, she didn't allow me to play.

I envisioned a picture a family friend sent to me. When I opened the text message, it read, *I remember you being so shy and not wanting to play.*

I examined the picture for several minutes and felt like I was that little girl again. I sit with my mother, watching other kids play. I watched everyone have fun while I sat quietly, wishing I could play along with everyone. I didn't respond to that message because I didn't want to reveal that I didn't choose to sit at that table.

I had to think about answering truthfully when the life coach asked if I was indeed an introvert. Instead, I sat back and stared straight at her, dumbfounded. I couldn't believe it was a possibility I wasn't an introvert. I had to ask what an introvert is to determine whether her statement was accurate. At this point, the life coach bothered me because she pointed out a flaw I couldn't foresee.

An introvert is a reflective, shy, reticent, reserved, or quiet person who enjoys spending time alone. Therefore, I had to ask myself, was that me? My honest answer was yes, but as a kid, I felt I had no choice but to spend time alone. Due to my mother's strict rules, I didn't have many friends.

Not that I didn't have any because I had them in school. I struggled when I received an invitation to a classmate's birthday party or wanted to play with neighborhood kids. For my mother to say yes, I had to figure out how to ask her. My expectation was always that the answer would be no. Sometimes, I didn't even ask because I knew she wouldn't let me go anywhere.

After that, I explored the meaning of being an introvert in more detail. Then, to determine whether my characteristics match those of an introvert, I read about the characteristics of an introvert. Having an introverted personality can be both natural and nurturing. So, even though I wasn't born this way, it was something I became due to my environment.

After several sessions with Kendra, I felt I didn't know myself. She would ask me hard questions, which weren't right or wrong answers, to help me figure out who I was.

"Tell me more about your mother, Janell," Kendra said.

In my mind, I remembered all the times my mother stood in the way of me doing something I wanted to do. She had negative comments that prevented me from even attempting it.

A few examples of negative comments have stuck with me throughout these years since I was a child. One year, a cousin of mine participated in a beauty pageant. She won Ms. Photogenic, which was fascinating.

"Can I join the contest next year?" I asked.

"Why? You are too fat and not pretty enough," Mom responded.

I put my head down, and she continued to say, "If your cousin couldn't make it and only received Ms. Photogenic, what makes you think you would win?"

"Those were cruel words to say to anyone," Kendra said.

I tried defending my mother by saying, "I believed she didn't want me to fail. She didn't want to see me go through humiliation."

Kendra's facial expressions were a little disturbing, but I told her my childhood stories.

In my mind, a beauty contest wouldn't help me become anyone in this world, so I only had one other option: school. At the very least, I needed to ensure high grades. Yet, semester after semester, all I heard was that my grades weren't good at all. I could have had all A's and B's, but it wasn't good enough for my mother. She would then use the B's as an excuse to keep me from participating in any activities besides attending church.

What would I excel at if I were not smart enough? Is there a purpose to my existence? In addition to not being pretty and skinny, I was also not intelligent.

I would spend endless hours playing solitaire with physical cards or writing. I mainly wrote about my imaginary friends or the life I would have had if I had been born into a different family. I use my imagination all the time. I wished I could have saved those stories because I would have been an author ages ago. I would rip them up and throw them away once I finished writing them. There was a fear that someone would read them and say they weren't good enough.

Sometimes, the answer would be no, even if my older brother asked me to play outside. Her reason was that it was all boys, and girls didn't belong with the boys. So, my brother spent much of his time outside the apartment while I suffered inside.

I couldn't even talk to her because most of the time, she had an attitude because I would stay mute. The only time I spoke was when I was in school. As I got older, it was tough for me to communicate with anyone. I would get such anxiety when I felt anyone giving me eye contact.

I also didn't know how to process my emotions. When someone gave me constructive criticism, I would tear up. When I was in pain, I would laugh. But, in the aftermath of someone's death, I was numb.

With all the information I just provided, Kendra gave me an assignment. She wanted me to write a letter to my younger self.

"What should I write about?" I asked.

"Anything from your past that you couldn't control, so you can let it go," she paused and waited to see if I could answer any questions.

"Write anything that comes to mind and then read it aloud. Then, you can burn it or share it with me if you wish."

I looked at her as if she were crazy. *Why do I want to write a letter to my younger self? How will this help me?* Since I'm a good student, I did the assignment.

I wanted to research more about what we discussed in our session. So, I tried to read through all the characteristics since I realized my environment caused me to be an introvert. So, I looked it up on many websites. You can find more information about this characteristic at verywellmind.com.

1. Being around a lot of people drains your energy.
2. You enjoy solitude.
3. You have a small group of friends.
4. People may find it challenging to get to know you.
5. Too much stimulation leaves you feeling distracted.
6. You are very self-aware.
7. You like to learn by watching.
8. Jobs that involve independence draw you in.

Whether it's fortunate or unfortunate, I possess all these characteristics. Growing up, I spent a lot of time alone, so it's easy to understand why I would be an introvert. However, while researching, I also wanted to learn how to stop being an introvert. The website verywellmind.com (2022) states that introverts cannot stop being introverts, but there are other things they can do to control themselves.

So, I sat and stared at a blank piece of paper. I didn't want to write to my younger self. I didn't want to accept Kendra's statement or what I'd read. So, I became defiant. That's when I knew I would see more of Kendra.

CHAPTER 13

SHOOTING

Every single muscle in my body is tight and rigid. I feel stiff.

Whenever I have to attend an event with my husband, my anxiety shifts into high gear. Anxious because I don't know how the night will play out. I always have to be on guard for any possible scenario with him. Any fighting. Any attitude. Anything.

Because I strive to avoid any unfavorable outcome, I constantly second-guess any invitation from anyone. But we received an invitation to a graduation party for a friend's son. This event occurred at a popular strip restaurant in Orlando. Yes, a large amount of alcohol is involved!

Upon entering, music was playing, and bright lights and neon signs were hanging from the ceiling with funny quotes. Tables are arranged more abstractly than in any particular order. At the front, there is a stage with a DJ playing and ready to party. Waiters and waitresses run the restaurant floor to ensure everyone is cared for with food and drinks. In addition, there are small stages in the restaurants where you can jump up and dance if you wish.

As soon as we passed the front line, they checked our IDs and gave us a bracelet based on age. Looking around the room, we tried to locate our friends. Our eyes caught sight of their table, so we walked over. There were about twenty people at our party. My husband and I brought my niece to go out for the night. She was only nineteen years old at the time. After 11:00 p.m. it was a requirement for everyone under twenty-one to leave.

We mingled with everyone and ordered our food. Every time we visited this restaurant, we requested the same meals, so there was no need to look at the menus. As we sat and waited for our food, the drinks started coming in. Throughout the night, I took pictures and videos of what was happening to avoid paying too much attention to the drinks.

The live DJ and the staff do everything to have the audience entertained and involved throughout the night. This particular night my friend's mother, Melva, decided to join the dance competition they usually hold at the restaurant. She isn't a shy lady at all. She was the only big older woman on stage competing against three skinny young girls for a shot for the entire table. We were ready to celebrate and watch her take the crown from these young girls.

They didn't know what they signed up for going against Melva. She climbed up onto that stage and shook every inch of her body. Anything that could jiggle was surely jiggling, and Melva was very proud of it all. She wasn't the only one proud because our whole table was screaming, clapping, yelling, and cheering her on. Not only did we want the free shot, but she is so much fun that we wanted her to continue kicking these young girls' asses.

As the night progressed, I wasn't paying attention to what Carlos was doing in the restaurant, which was surprising because I usually would, but we were all having such a good time that it didn't matter. A few of our party decided to leave when it was time for just twenty-one and over. Okay, so it will be time for us to leave because we have our niece with us. I looked over, and my niece had a different color bracelet.

"Wait, where did you get that from?" I asked.

"Tio got it for me," Nana responded. In case you didn't know, Tio means uncle in Spanish.

I walked over to my husband to ask what was happening, and he was smiling.

"I don't want to leave, so I asked the waiter if he could find me the bracelet for Nana," my husband explained. The waiter wasn't being nice just to be nice. My husband sure did give him a great tip.

As for drinking, I would not allow Nana to do so, and she was not interested in drinking either. Because we were all having such a good time, my husband didn't want to end the night early. If necessary, I could use her as the designated driver, but I have my limit, so I know I can drive since my husband was well over his limit. All these years, we've had the same rule with one another. I knew I would drive if he drank heavily. He was responsible for driving if I wanted to drink more than usual.

We danced the night away with the crew that stood behind us. Mickey, at the time my Nina's boyfriend, was dancing on the small stage. Between him and my husband, I think our tab for the night was about $1,000. Yes, they can drink. My tab may have been less than $30, which included food because I didn't drink much. I was recording, dancing, and taking pictures.

As the night got closer to the end, I asked my husband to get our check. It was my way of telling him to start wrapping it up.

We were all so happy. I was at peace that nothing had happened to ruin our night. Then, Carlos, Nana, and I started walking toward the car parked behind the building, so it was a little walk. It was dark, but nothing abnormal, and nothing felt unsafe since so many people walked toward their cars.

Well, we all get into the car. I'm driving, my husband is the passenger, and my niece sits in the back seat. I looked in the rearview mirror to ensure she was okay and in the car so that I could take off. I pulled out of the parking lot and headed toward the highway.

I announced in the car, "I'm going to drop you off first, and then I'll drop Nana off and head home." At this point in our relationship, we weren't living together, and his apartment was the furthest from mine. So, in my head, it just made sense to drop him off first.

However, after stating my plan, I saw that my husband's attitude had changed. "What's wrong?" I asked. He didn't respond to my question, so I just let it be. He seemed bothered and angry about something, and we all rode quietly, just listening to music.

As I jumped off the highway to take the local streets toward Carlos's apartment, I noticed he had reached into my glove compartment. He placed the gun there earlier in the evening. A few hand movements drew my attention, so I looked at him. As he checked the magazine of the gun, he cocked it back to load it. As I looked in the rearview mirror again, I noticed my niece's worried expression. Then, suddenly, my husband sticks his right arm out of the passenger window as I drive down the main road.

At this point, my mind was racing, and I had no idea what he was doing. Following the trigger pull and firing of the shots, I hear nothing more. While I was driving, he fired about six rounds. To ensure everything would be okay, I immediately disassociated myself from it all. Looking around, I ensured there were no cops and no one was out in the streets who might have gotten hurt. Then I looked back at my niece. I saw her eyes lock with mine. At this point, I knew I had to change plans and take her straight home.

"Carlos," I said so calmly. I didn't get a negative response from him. I wasn't sure if he could turn the gun at himself or me, so I didn't want to give it any more reaction. "Really?"

Five minutes later, I went to my niece's apartment to drop her off. I kissed her and made sure she made it in fine. Then, I drove off, and the next stop was Carlos's apartment.

We didn't speak, and I had the music turned off. I tried to drive as fast as possible without getting stopped by the cops, but I just wanted to relieve myself from having Carlos in my car. I wasn't nervous at all, but I wanted him out. I didn't know what his next move was. When I disassociate, I don't have a big reaction to anything. It's more of getting me to a safe place so I can react. My goal was to drop him off. We finally got to his destination. I usually wait until he walks toward his door for me to drive us, but I didn't care if he made it in safely this time. I just wanted to leave.

I drove out of his complex onto his main road. I looked at all my mirrors to check my surroundings. Five minutes later, my tears started rolling down my face. I told myself not to cry because I needed to make it home safely.

After a fifteen-minute ride in my thoughts, I made it to my apartment. I lay down on my bed in disbelief as to what had just happened. I was still in disassociation mode, and I couldn't react. I just lay on the bed, processing the events. I tried to figure out what had happened and why Carlos could do such a thing.

It was about 1:30 a.m. when I texted my friend Nina.

"Girl, I'm done."

Without knowing what happened, she responded, "I'm sure."

"With Carlos," I stated because I wasn't sure if she knew I was talking about him.

"I know what you meant. My Mr. is effed up, and when the air hit him," she responded with the little emoji of a head exploding. But, of course, since everyone around me knows Carlos had an issue with medication and drinking, I could only imagine she thought I was just saying he was drunk.

"Carlos shot out of my car."

"Oh, no way," she responded.

I knew I didn't want to speak on the phone, but I needed to vent it out to someone, so I could snap out of my current state and finally react. I just couldn't react. I fell asleep but woke up to myself crying. I cried because everything was going so well that night. I thought we were going to end the night with no issues. It wasn't the case at all.

I reached out to a few of my friends to vent the next day. Everyone I spoke to was shocked, and no one knew what advice to give me. I didn't know how I would handle the situation either. I opted to relax by getting my manicure and pedicure, hoping I could finally face the situation and call Carlos. I walked out of my apartment and sat in my car. I looked over to the passenger seat where Carlos was sitting last night.

A bullet shell casing was sitting on the seat in plain sight. Seeing this casing made me react how I expected myself to react when everything happened. I grabbed the shell casing, took a picture, and sent it to him. At this point, I was so upset because he could have killed any of us. He could have killed anyone walking down the street or in someone's home. I finally felt panic. The fear. The disappointment. I finally felt the emotions. My whole body started shaking, and my tears rushed out of my eyeballs.

I took a picture and texted it to Carlos with the words, "Why?" I wanted to know why he did something that could have forever changed our lives.

"I don't know," Carlos responded. He usually doesn't recall why he does what he does.

After years of research and speaking to different individuals, I have learned that it comes with the territory of the illness. For example, Carlos's doctors had to explain to me that someone diagnosed with manic depression, like Carlos, will do things they will not remember later on.

Dr. Horn gave me an example of a happily married woman, but she would go out and have affairs when she was in a manic episode. Her husband would find out about them, and he had the choice of staying or leaving, but he would forgive her and be by her side because he knew it was her illness, not her.

It was very hard to comprehend that you will hurt so much because someone you love cannot control themselves. Although someone battling a mental illness doesn't want to hurt you, the illness takes over.

While writing this book, I started listening to different podcasts to understand the perspective of someone with an illness. As much as I wanted to accept certain actions, I needed to hear from someone else. I came across a podcaster by the name of Gabe Howard. He has a podcast called *A Bipolar, A Schizophrenic, and a Podcast.*

I reached out to him, and he accepted my request for an interview. At the beginning of the interview, I discussed how Carlos shot out of my car, and he couldn't provide a reason. Gabe's response was very eye-opening for me, and I'm sure it will be eye-opening for you. Below is his response to why Carlos did not know why he shot out my car window:

Gabe Howard: *He may never know why. I'm in a fortunate position, and I reached recovery. I've been stable for a very long time. And with my job, I get to dive back into the past and rehash all this stuff.*

I wanted to jump, and people were cheering, so I did.

I don't consider jumping off a roof a good thing. People were around, and I was on a rooftop, so I jumped. I didn't die. So, it wasn't like a thirty-story roof. The lawn was kind of squishy. I was a fat guy. I was also young, you know, I was like twenty-five years old. So, I'm sure if I did that now at forty-five, I would break every bone in my body.

But whatever.

As I saw the next day, there wasn't any lasting damage. But we still have to wonder. People are asking, how did you know you'd be okay? No, I didn't consider that part. Look, I was lucky. It was a garage roof, its slope, the height, less than a story. But I got a running jump again as a fat guy. I mean, I weighed, like, 400–500 pounds when this happened.

So, there are a lot of blubbers to catch my fall. The ground was kind of mushy grass but not mud, but soft. It wasn't frozen, solid tundra. And it all worked out.
But that could have quickly gone a million different ways. I had to leap over the side, and I could have tripped when I jumped, landed headfirst on the sidewalk, and died instantly. But, on the other hand, I could have landed weirdly and broken my leg.

There are a million things that could have happened. Several people have asked me whether I will be okay, but I have never considered it. I just jumped. There are plenty of other ways that it could have turned out. It was a mess. But here we are. And I'm happy that it worked out. But then the point is, they are unknowable. I have tried so hard to ask all the people around me about it so that I can understand it. But ultimately, I don't know why I jumped off the roof. That's just the answer.

Just like that, I had to move on.

CHAPTER 14

THIRTY-EIGHT

What is the difference between a thirty-seven-year-old versus a thirty-eight-year-old? Every year I do a self-analyzation. I think about life and purpose. I look at myself and ask, where have all the years gone? Today, November 7, 2018, I turn thirty-eight. I didn't think anything would be different or unique because I didn't expect anything from anyone. I shared that day with my mother from a young age, so I didn't make a huge deal. Her birthday was a day before mine.

The biggest reason I'm not particularly eager to celebrate my birthday is that I need to learn to embrace the attention given during the celebration. There was no point in my life I could recall a celebration for any birthdates, accomplishments, or milestones. Every day was just a regular day for us in the household. We were just lucky to survive another day in our world. So now, as an adult, it is challenging to celebrate anything good in life.

Celebrating the day with others is more attention focused on me, which I shy away from for several reasons, such as social anxiety and fear of criticism. So, I didn't do much to celebrate myself throughout all these years. So, I planned to grab some food, go to the DMV to renew my plates, and then get a massage. I wanted to go out on the massage with CBD oil and other relaxing oils. Pamper me and spend the day with me like any other day. Unfortunately, before things went as planned, there was a snag.

Here in Florida, our license plate sticker expires on our birthday. Yes, I always wait until the last minute, which I'm trying to get better at, but I wouldn't say I like the DMV. Carlos's vehicle was solely under my name, and my vehicle had both of our names on the title. My name is primary on my vehicle, so the DMV uses my birthdate for registration. Also, before purchasing our sticker, we must ensure we don't have any outstanding tolls. I expected to have some on my car, and I was always afraid to see how many tolls Carlos had not paid.

As expected, Carlos had many tolls on his vehicle. We needed to pay the tolls before obtaining the sticker. Since I, of course, was the one that ended up being responsible, I had the money to pay for it. We both worked, but Carlos isn't a planner and tends to spend money as it comes in. He has always been one who never worries about the future but more about today. So, if he had $500 in his account today in his head, he could spend those $500 right away. He doesn't have the mentality that tomorrow isn't a promise, so why hold onto money?

I surely didn't want to pay his debt, but I had no other choice in this case. I wanted my sticker. He never saved money to cover these situations, which drove me crazy.

Calling different departments of the DMV to get everything cleared didn't start my day how I wished. I'm annoyed at this point. Then if I mention anything to him, I'm always making him feel bad. So as always, I considered his feeling and tried to keep them to myself.

After getting everything squared away, I got the massage I had scheduled for my birthday. While I was there, the massage therapist suggested I use CBD oil with my massage for extra relaxation. The massage therapist instructed me not to shower so the CBD oil could soak into my skin. Instead, the massage therapist suggested I walk around greasy from head to toe. I didn't think anything of it, so I agreed. I left my massage with my skin greased up and hair that looked like I had not washed it in several weeks.

I had to rush to the DMV to pick up the stickers since they didn't want to give them to Carlos. As mentioned before, Carlos's name wasn't on his vehicle, so legally, they couldn't give Carlos the sticker for his vehicle. I communicated with him throughout the process, but I was very annoyed with this whole process.

My annoyance is that if he had been responsible enough to take care of his tolls and vehicle, I wouldn't have had to deal with all this on my birthday and would have had more time to focus on myself. I tried to snap out of it because Carlos had already told me he was to take me out to eat. I was okay with going out, but I didn't think I wasn't going to be able to take a shower. I didn't want to cancel on him, so I still went, but I needed to put more effort into making myself look great.

The second snag was about the restaurant of choice. Carlos's first suggestion was a Mexican restaurant near my apartment. This restaurant has a live DJ on certain days to make the environment more upbeat. However, I didn't want to go because I'd been there plenty of times. Also, it's my birthday, so I wanted to try something different.

Carlos felt I was trying to avoid the restaurant location because I didn't want to cross paths with someone I knew. It got me frustrated because everyone knows I like to try new places and new things. But Carlos has always been so suspicious of this Mexican restaurant. His suspicion started when he accused me of going on a date with a guy to this particular restaurant.

I recall exactly when it happened, but I had the choice to either be truly honest or avoid answering his question. In the past, I had always answered based on a person's demeanor. But first, I needed to make sure I was safe.

A few months before my birthday, Carlos walked into my apartment. I already felt the negative vibe. I immediately got defensive and braced myself for what was to come. Then, I waited for him to start the conversation.

"I don't want to argue, but I want you to tell me the truth," Carlos said.

I looked at him with my mind racing because I knew if I told him the truth, he wouldn't believe me, so I knew this would turn into an argument.

"You posted the video on social media, and I passed by the restaurant and saw you were sitting in the front booth with a guy and another couple," Carlos continued without interrupting. "You were on a double date."

I couldn't help but giggle because, through all these years, he doesn't seem even to know how I look for him to think any other female was me. I told him I was not sitting in the front booth but toward the back of the restaurant near the bathroom, where I was standing while recording the kids. The reaction I gave him seemed to bother him even more.

"I was asked to hang out at the restaurant since several people I knew through networking were hanging out."

I recorded some kids dancing to the DJ's music that night. I posted that recording on social media, and Carlos saw it. I wasn't hiding anything and didn't think there would be any issue with me being there since it was all innocent. However, that wasn't the case.

So, I don't know if he drove past, but I know for sure I was not on a double date or even a date, for that matter.

"I need the truth, Janell," Carlos said.

His tone of voice elevated, and his body movement toward me got aggressive. His chest puffed up, and I saw his hands ball into a fist. I got scared. As much as I wanted to be honest with him, all my nerves kicked in. I started to envision all the adverse outcomes that could happen if I told him the truth.

I feared for my safety. Suddenly, my mind went blank. I felt lost. I don't know what was beginning to happen to me. I was looking straight at Carlos but felt like I was standing over the both of us, just watching us from afar. I've officially felt disconnected from this conversation.

Carlos has never been physical with me, but his actions toward me or around me can be very frightening. So, I explained the false answer, but he didn't believe me.

My defense mechanism throughout my years here on earth is basically to disassociate from high-pressure situations. The best way I can describe myself disassociating is like an out-of-body experience. Although I'm physically present and hear everything, my response may not be customary for the specific situation.

I also may need to remember everything that happened after I stopped disassociating from the event. Some people call it blacking out. So, when I saw him upset and expressing himself, I couldn't help but giggle. I knew I shouldn't have laughed, but I couldn't help but do so. I do this naturally to keep calm and brace myself for any possible outcome. The result is going to be very damaging. I felt disassociated from this conversation.

I could tell him the truth. A male friend came into town from Chicago, and we went to hang out and catch up on life. I knew he would start asking for names and assume the worst, so instead, I gave him a different answer.

"You think I'm stupid?" Carlos said. He continued saying, "You think I don't know my wife?"

As I sat on my sofa, waiting for him to finish his rant, I could think he didn't know me. He couldn't tell if I was the one sitting in a booth with another couple or not. I don't know if I was in disbelief or mad. I couldn't make out my emotions at the time.

He was so upset that he grabbed a cigarette and went to my balcony to smoke. I used this as an opportunity to lie on my sofa and close my eyes. When I reopened my eyes, I realized I had fallen asleep. I don't know how long I was sleeping, but he was sitting on the other side of the sofa watching TV. He waited until I woke up. I prayed to myself that this argument was over. I couldn't take the pressure anymore. I hated arguing with him, or anyone for that matter. I didn't want it to escalate, so I took myself out of the problem by just going to sleep. The negative energy and the arguing just drained me.

Ever since this argument, he tried different reasons for us to go to this restaurant, but I refused. So, when he suggested it for my birthday, it wasn't because I wanted to avoid it but because I wanted to try something new.

I'm all about experiencing new places and creating new memories. So, we opted to go to the new establishment Carlos nor I had ever been to, but it wasn't a fancy place. It was an American food place with rock music in the background. All over the walls were rock bands that I didn't know since I don't listen to rock music. We knew many tourists would be there since it was near the airport. It didn't bother me since I love seeing and feeling new environments. People could take their pets and sit outside on the patio with their fur babies. I love to see that, but I couldn't take our fur babies because one will have anxiety, and the other will be hyper. The way I was dressed, I just wanted to be laid back.

What I didn't know was that he invited other people to attend. He invited several people, but only four showed up. From my understanding, he asked my friend Ely and her three kids, Iris and her two kids, and Nina, her boyfriend, and her three kids. He also invited our compadres Junior and Vani and their three kids. He was upset because I am always helping everyone, but when it comes to me, no one comes through for me. He didn't express this to me, but he did say it to my friend Nina. He called her and was highly upset that they all backed out on my birthday celebration.

"Are you going to make it today?" Carlos asked Nina.

"Yes," she responded but was confused about why he would be asking.

He stated that my other friends, which are so-called sisters, all backed out, so they were not going to make it. This agitated him. He says, "She is always there for all of them, and no one could be here for her." Carlos proceeded to speak and excuse my French but his words, "Fuck them all."

Nina was one friend that always showed up. No matter the situation, she would always make it unless she was out of town, which was rare on special occasions.

Carlos and I separated for about two years at this point. However, he kept in contact and still was around because he wanted our family back. We attended birthdays, holidays, and family gatherings together, but everyone knew we weren't living together. When I say he wanted our family back, it was me, him, and our fur babies Dulce and Bam Bam.

He was stern about not giving me a divorce, and I never pushed for it because I thought about him. I sincerely believed that maybe one day we would get back together, but he needed to get his life together and be happy before we could be together.

Carlos went out of his way to plan a birthday gathering. I never expected him to ever do this for me. He was so happy while I was feeling uncomfortable. I felt uncomfortable because of the snags throughout the day, which involved him and other things that had nothing to do with him. I wasn't happy with myself. My life was stressful, and his actions didn't help.

We sat and talked with our friends while having dinner and a few drinks. Everything that happened throughout the day didn't matter anymore. I was enjoying the moment.

My friend had placed a gift bag under the table. I didn't realize it was down there, so I turned my body, which made my leg shift, and hit the gift bag. Hitting the bag made it tilt over. The gift she purchased was some glass candle holders that broke. There were three in all, but two survived. I felt so bad because I knew she had gone to get me something for my apartment. In my defense, I didn't realize the bag was under the table.

One of my cousins, who had just moved to Orlando, also showed up while we ate. I was surprised because I had not seen her for a while. Also a little embarrassed because I'm not too fond of attention, and she is loud, which had everyone looking at us. At one point, our waiter told us to go outside. I thought he was kicking us out from the inside dining room because my cousin was so loud with how she spoke. It embarrassed me.

Much to my surprise, they had a cake waiting for me on the outside patio. Everyone started singing happy birthday to me. I was in shock. He made sure to get the custom cake I wanted. It was more of a cookie shaped in a big thirty-eight with flowers and chocolate placed on the pretty cake. My smile was so big because I didn't expect it at all. I was looking so crazy because I had a massage with CBD oil that I couldn't wash off earlier that day. I seriously did not dress for the occasion.

I had put my hair up in a messy bun and wore a black fitted T-shirt and yoga pants. I had no makeup on at all. My sideburns needed waxing. I looked crazy like I had just rolled out of bed and walked out of my apartment. Although I was excited, I was also embarrassed because I should have made an effort to look presentable.

But in my defense, I did not expect this. I looked back on the video they recorded, singing me happy birthday, and saw I didn't even hug my husband. He held and kissed me on my head several times, but I was looking at the cake.

Even though I was delighted, I didn't show too many emotions.

CHAPTER 15

RESENTMENT

"Oh my God, it is great to see you!" Kendra said.

We smile at each other and embrace one another. It has been a while since I had last seen Kendra. There was a lot I needed to get off my chest.

She asked, "How's it going?"

With a smile, I said, "It's going!"

"What's new, tell me?"

"Well, I need some help. I moved out of our apartment a few months back and have been living alone ever since."

There was a complete look of shock on her face. "Are you divorcing?" she asked.

"No, but I asked him several times for a divorce, and he said no."

"He doesn't have any control over it."

As far as I knew, Carlos's attempt to hold on offered some hope to us.

My heart broke when she said, "It's okay to divorce." She looked at me without emotion. "Give each other time to fix yourselves, and then if you want to try again, you can always remarry."

Remarry?

I thought to myself for a second, and remarrying isn't an option for me. Divorce is the end of our relationship. But, for me, there is no turning back. As a result of the lack of reciprocation I have received throughout my marriage, I am numb.

"Janell," she said. She tried to bring me back to our session after I spaced out in thought.

"Yes," I said as I looked at her.

"I want to know what's going on in your mind right now."

As a result of all that had happened, I was hesitant to share my thoughts with her. *Should I lie? Should I tell her the truth?* With my eyes on my lap, I couldn't find the words to describe my feelings.

"Okay, how did you feel when I said divorced?" Kendra asked.

No response from my end.

"In our last session, we discussed your mother. Would you like to explain your relationship with Carlos?"

With tears, I explained how I never wanted to feel again. In the last few years of our marriage, I did not feel sexually desired by Carlos. Carlos did not seem to be interested in me.

Our relationship began purely sexually. Before I met Carlos, I was in a dark place, and my outlet was having sex. I wasn't interested in relationships, so it was all sex. I had sex with guys I didn't even know, but at the moment, it released the endorphins I needed. After that, I felt horrible about myself until I slept with someone else.

For several years, I excused my behavior, saying I was single and it didn't matter since I wasn't hurting anyone. At that time, I worked full time and attended school full time, so I had no time for relationships. However, it was meeting Carlos that prevented me from continuing my addiction.

He wasn't going to be any different from any of the other guys until he was because he fed my addiction. Now I didn't have to jump from guy to guy. I had just one person to give me what I needed. We had always joked that he was just my summer fling. I had the summer off to grieve my cousin's and uncle's deaths, so he was my partner for the time being. I thought I wouldn't have time for him once I returned to my classes. That didn't happen because he stuck around.

After Carlos failed to provide me with sexual satisfaction, I began to feel unwanted. That desire was no longer present in his eyes. I wondered if I was too fat and too ugly for him. I gained so much weight, and anything I did wasn't helping me lose weight. He was also depressed due to his inability to be as active as before due to his spine injury. His depression and my insecurities were challenging to deal with simultaneously, but we did our best. Or maybe we ignored it all and pretended we weren't having problems.

Unfortunately, we were young and didn't receive guidance on how to handle our relationship.

Drug abuse and a lack of affection continued. Once I lost weight, I thought Carlos would be interested in me. I hired a personal trainer, started eating healthy, and worked out outside every day. To be healthy with Carlos, I changed my lifestyle. It was significant to me that he was proud of me. Carlos should feel proud to say I am his wife.

With the health journey, I was harsh on myself that I lost so much weight it looked like I was just all boobs and head. It wasn't until he showed me a picture of myself that I realized it. I had significant body dysmorphia.

Body dysmorphia is a mental illness involving obsessive focus on a perceived flaw in appearance. As a child, when my mother would say I was fat and ugly, I created this obsession.

My body dysmorphism continued into adulthood when I was in a relationship with Carlos. He never thought I was pretty enough for him. As a result, I hated taking pictures and hiding because I didn't want to see how disgusting I looked. Due to this obsession, I lost years of memories.

Carlos would always get so upset with me because there were times when I would change countless times and cry. Since I was uncomfortable in my skin, I didn't want to go anywhere. Even though I was sick then, it didn't help that my husband would wait months without even touching me, which further intensified my self-destruction.

Since he was addicted to his medication and always in pain, I would brush it off as his illness kept him from seeking me out sexually. However, the more I made excuses for him, the less I felt like a woman.

My mother was right. I was incapable of being competent at anything other than being a whore. When I was sleeping around, I was most productive and had what I wanted, a successful career, a successful education, and good health. But, as a wife, I was fat, unsightly, then too skinny, without a job, and with no goals. It felt like I was stuck. Every morning I cried and told myself to get out of my funk.

While Carlos slept, I would look at him and say I couldn't help him. It was time for me to help myself. So, I started doing fast cardio in our complex. As a result, my mood improved, and my image improved as well. The size of my body fluctuated over the years, so I had to find out what worked for me.

Occasionally, I would get out of the shower and walk around naked. Carlos would not bat an eye. As we had been without sex for a while, I decided to keep track without telling him.

As the months passed, I was unaware I was catching other men's attention. I tried to ignore that for many years to be a faithful wife. The pain in my heart grew with every passing month. The only thing Carlos cared about was his drugs.

One morning, I had to wake up early because I was attending a networking event. As soon as I woke up, Carlos wasn't in the room. I walked downstairs to look for him and found that all the doors in our house were open, including the garage door. In our driveway, I saw Carlos sitting in our pickup truck. I walked outside to see what he was doing.

The truck's hood and the driver's door were open, and his leg was sticking out. His head was leaning back on the seat as he snored loudly with his mouth open. His lap caught my attention. He wore blue latex gloves and held a gun in his right hand. While it was unclear what he was planning to do, my first instinct was to grab the gun and hide it inside.

As I walked upstairs to get ready, I felt furious. Because I had a networking event to attend, I couldn't show my emotions. How much more can I take of this shit? Once I had finished getting ready, I woke him up and forced him inside. After closing everything up, I drove away.

I'm just his fucking caregiver, were my thoughts while I sat at the event. Despite wanting to get out, I didn't want to go home, so I sat quietly, wishing the time would pass quickly. After I left, I drove around to decompress and figure out my next move with his man. Being a great wife is nearly impossible when your husband isn't great.

After a couple of weeks, I received a message from someone I barely knew but was friends with on social media. Carlos and I were sleeping in separate rooms at this point. To keep his identity private, I will use the name Juan. I was curious about what Juan wanted of me, so I entertained the conversation. He admitted to me that he was interested in me. His admission shocked me because of my lack of self-confidence. The conversation ended when I told him I was still with Carlos, which he respected.

After a few months, Juan reached out again. I was furious with Carlos because he continued to do things that jeopardized our relationship, so I entertained the conversation.

"I'll be in Orlando in a couple of days."

"For how long?" I asked.

He would be in town for five days for work and hoping to see me. I initially refused because I didn't want anything to happen. Finally, on his last day in town, I reached out to him and told him I would take him up on his offer.

My body started shaking, and I was terrified. *What the hell are you doing?* But it didn't stop me. I showed up where he was staying. I didn't know where to meet him, so I called him.

"I'm here. Where are you?" I asked.

"Park on the right side of the building so no one will see you," he stated.

Even though no one knew me there, I believed he was still trying to protect us. Carlos could get crazy, and he didn't want me to get into any more trouble.

Despite my trembling, I get out of my car as he walks to it. He hugged me and felt how nervous I was at that moment.

"It's okay," he said.

It had been almost a year since I had sex, let alone with someone else. I stood there about to commit a sin I had always vowed never to commit. However, as a Catholic, guilt was a part of my upbringing.

The first thing I did when we entered his room was sit on the couch. I saw his suitcase on the ground with his belongings packed away. I glanced over to the bed and thought he was the right person.

He didn't live here, and there would be no strings attached, and no one would ever know. Taking hold of my hand, he helped me from the couch to the bed. We both started getting undressed. I looked at him and said, "Let's do this fast because I have to leave."

He laughed at me, picked me up, and threw me on the bed.

As we were having sex, I didn't experience any guilt. It all felt right. The hands of a man touched my naked body.

Oh shit, I didn't even shave my legs. The hairs weren't long, but my legs weren't smooth either.

"I'm so sorry, I didn't shave my legs," I said.

He, indeed, didn't care about the prickly legs. He told me how beautiful I looked and how great I felt. I soaked it all in. I loved every moment of it. Finally, I looked at the clock and told him to hurry up because I had to run. Then I washed up, dressed, and rushed out.

While driving home, I could only think that I didn't even kiss Juan. I didn't notice my nerves because it was pure sex. At this point, I didn't care what Carlos thought. So, as I drove home, I just smiled.

When I walked in, he was high, just as I had suspected. Neither he nor I said anything to each other. There was an air of indifference about my absence. I walked up the stairs and headed for the bathroom. Standing there staring at the shower, I let out a cry. I cried not because of what I did but because I felt angry. It made me mad that my husband didn't care where I was or who I was with because, once again, he was high and in his world.

All these years, I had put a lot of value on myself, and I did the exact opposite, and I was not remorseful. Angry at Carlos, I slammed the door to my bathroom so hard. Because of all the shit he has put me through, I am now resentful. I have become the woman my mother always said I would be.

I was now a whore.

Kendra's voice snapped me back into the present time.

"Janell, was that the only time you cheated on him?"

CHAPTER 16

I DID IT AGAIN

"Honestly, no, that wasn't the only time I've cheated," I responded. I looked up at her waiting for her to pass judgment on me.

"Would you like to tell me about the next time?" she asked with no facial expression. It didn't surprise her at all.

"It was with a different person, and it lasted longer," I explained.

"Okay, start from the beginning."

As my business grew, I faced the realities of building my brand. I am the face of my company, so I need professional headshots. I dreaded this because my negative side kicked in and destroyed any ounce of self-motivation.

Thoughts began to pop into my head, such as:

1. I need to be better to be doing this work.
2. The amount of intelligence I possess is insufficient.

3. The insecurities about my appearance.
4. Why would anyone choose me to handle their accounting or taxes?

One afternoon, I received an email inquiring about my services. *Janell, you can handle this.* I usually give myself a small pep talk before I reach out to a prospect. The following are the steps I take:

1. Contact the potential client
2. Determine what they need
3. Book an in-person meeting
4. Review any documents

I completed steps one through three, leaving step four, praying that they would become my clients. When I walked into his office, I had new business clothes and a new sense of confidence. I did not even recognize myself. *I have to play a part since these people don't know me.*

"Hello, I'm looking for Chris," I asked the first person I saw.

"Chris!" he shouted.

As he walked over to me, I could tell he was nervous. While he was trying to explain his situation to me, I couldn't help but laugh because he couldn't even look me in the eye. Next, I scanned the room to see if anyone else had noticed what I had witnessed. Since no one was paying attention, I focused back on him.

"Why do you think he was nervous?" Kendra asked.

"Since I was a child, I could tell my mother's feelings. Now that I'm an adult, I use that ability."

"Interesting."

Chris's body language indicated that he found me attractive, but he knew it was wrong because I was there for work. We continued our conversation, and I promised to send him a proposal for the work I think he needs. However, due to his poor emailing skills, he recommended I return in person. As a result, we set up a time and date.

A week had passed, and it was the day of our appointment. Unfortunately, I just realized I had my professional headshot photoshoot scheduled for the same day. Since I didn't know how to do hair and makeup, I hired an on-site makeup artist.

When the photoshoot was over, I looked in the mirror and hated how I looked. The makeup artist teased my hair so high and put pounds of foundation on my face that it felt heavy. As soon as the photographer saw I wasn't happy with the look, she explained that she could soften the makeup and edit my hair.

I followed her instructions since she was a professional. I felt ugly the entire time. Damn it, and I let those negative thoughts creep back into my head. *Janell, stop it!* I kept telling myself. After the session, she showed me the unedited version of the photos so I could choose which ones I wanted. There was nothing I liked about any of them.

The experience left me feeling horrible about myself. I wasn't sure if it was my body dysmorphia or if the markup artist did an awful job. Since I lacked confidence in myself, I had to drop this proposal and find an excuse not to attend. Unfortunately, I was driving when a sudden storm hit.

Lord, thank you for providing me with this storm. Using the storm was the most appropriate excuse to skip the proposal delivery. Emailing him the document and calling him from there would be fine. It will prevent him or his employees from seeing me as a clown. Then, I can go home and wash my hair and face.

I walked into my home and looked at Carlos's face. His reaction wasn't surprising.

"What?" I asked him.

"Your hair is big," he replied.

"I know. I'm about to comb it out."

"You took pictures like that?"

I looked at him and just nodded my head, telling him yes. Great! As a result, I felt worse than ever.

While sitting at my dining room table, I emailed the proposal and called Chris. Unfortunately, it was still storming outside, so I used that as an excuse to cancel our meeting.

"Hello, Chris!"

"Hello, I thought you were coming today?" He questioned me quickly, which caught me by surprise.

"Yes, I planned on going, but I got caught in this storm, so I emailed it to you and wanted to set a time for us to review," I explained.

"Well, if we made an appointment for you to be here today, I expected it to happen with no excuses. A storm wouldn't stop you if you wanted the job so badly. I thought you were more professional than that."

This side of Chris wasn't the nervous side I met the other day. Instead, he made me feel precisely how my mother made me feel as a child. *He thought I was more professional* was a slap in my face. I thought for a second to come up with a response.

"I'll be there," I responded with a bit of shame.

As soon as I got up, I told Carlos I would be back. The opportunity to sign him as a client was too lucrative to pass up. The child in me came out and feared the tone of his voice. As I have done with my mother, I feared disappointing him. During the drive there, I mentally played the entire encounter. What I planned to say and what I didn't want to say. Once again, I felt like a child preparing to walk on eggshells. Getting clients isn't easy, but this is what I have to do—feeling humiliated and belittled for the sake of growing my business.

He seemed very cocky when I walked in. His behavior was all over the place. He was joking with people, speaking loudly, and was all over the place. Despite my attempts to review the proposal with him, he didn't seem interested. Sitting there, I stared at him, wondering what was going on. Before he even looked at my proposal, he asked when we would begin. We agreed on the date, and I did not question anything else. I was about to sign another paying client.

At this point, we had become friendly but had never crossed any boundaries since we were married. There would be occasional flirting, but it only boosted my ego. The only reason Chris was kind to me was that he liked me. He was disrespectful and just someone I would never even consider dating. As a result of his character, Chris was such an ugly person, but I took his compliments to heart since that was what I lacked at home. Despite a red flag waving, I ignored it because he was feeding me what I needed.

One day, sitting on my couch, I looked over at Carlos, who was sleeping. As we sat in the same room, I felt lonely. This loneliness wasn't the first time feeling this way. I often felt lonely, and the sad part was that Carlos was with me in my home. Carlos was so depressed that all he wanted to do was sleep. We barely spoke. We didn't have much money to do things. We didn't have sex. Shit, I don't even know what I was doing as a spouse, and I did not sign up to be his caregiver.

As I watched him sleep and heard him snore, I felt terrible for entertaining someone else, so I woke Carlos up. Then, due to our situation, I asked that we talk.

"We need to talk."

Looking at me, confused. "What about?" he asked.

"I need to know what is going on with us."

"What's going on?"

We just stared at each other for a few seconds. "I need to know if we plan to continue working on us."

"Of course."

I cried and begged him to talk because I was desperate. I didn't want us to fall apart. Carlos did what he always did. He sat there just quietly. Carlos watched me cry and pour my heart out to him. He gave me no reaction at all. The man was speechless and didn't know what to say. I felt like he didn't care about me or our relationship. What was the purpose of holding on?

Sitting on the sofa watching TV was the routine. He would fall asleep, and I would stay awake listening to the television while scrolling social media. I came across a post from Chris, which made me think of him. I looked over at Carlos, and he was on cloud nine. Nothing would wake him up.

I reached out to Chris and told him I wanted to see him. He was all up for it. We met up. We both knew we had to keep it a secret for ourselves and me. We didn't even talk. He led me to a room, and we quickly started to have sex. Afterward, I cleaned up and walked out. I sat in the car and remembered I didn't kiss him. I guess that's my thing. If I don't kiss you, then it doesn't mean anything.

"Did it end there?" Kendra asked.

CHAPTER 17

MY PUNISHMENT

With such shame, I couldn't lie to Kendra. So, I told her I continued an affair with Chris.

"Why do you think you continued this relationship?"

"Because he has been giving me what I've been missing for years?"

"Tell me about it."

After that first time with Chris, my desire to have sex intensified. Now I had a person of interest, and we were a great match. Both of us were married to someone who was ill. Neither of us wanted to leave our spouse, but both felt abandoned by them. We connected deeper due to the challenges of being a caregiver and sole provider. I did take a step back and focused on growing my business.

It had been months since I had paid attention to Chris. During that time, we still worked together and flirted occasionally, but nothing more serious. As long as we stayed cordial with one another and made working around each other comfortable, we maintained a distance.

A few months later, Carlos and I attended my niece's sweet sixteen. My self-confidence was high since I had already lost a lot of weight. My dress was lovely, and many people complimented me, which boosted my ego.

As the night passed and we were enjoying ourselves, I noticed we both had too much to drink. So, although I didn't care about stopping either, I did suggest to Carlos that we get a room and stay the night.

We inquired at the front desk if a room was available. Since we were both in a cheerful mood, I thought we would continue to have a great night. Carlos was all smiles as the night ended, which made me so happy. With so much excitement, we walked up to our room. We didn't plan to stay overnight or bring a just-in-case bag, so we'll sleep naked. As soon as I entered the room, I noticed two queen-sized beds.

As Carlos walked over to the bed on my right, he threw himself across it, leaving no space for me to lie down. I laughed as I asked him to take off his clothes so he wouldn't sleep in dress clothes. There was no sign that he was interested in removing his clothing or moving over to leave me space.

Tears flowed down my cheeks as I walked to the bathroom. After some time, I gathered my courage and took a picture of myself in the hotel mirror. Then, I looked over to Carlos as he lay there snoring.

Don't do it, Janell.

Despite knowing that what I was about to do wasn't right, I sent Chris that picture. I patiently waited for a response. He reacted as I expected.

"You look beautiful!"

"Thank you! It would have been great to have been there with you."

"Why, what's wrong?" he asked.

"Carlos is here, but like always, he didn't pay attention to me."

He didn't respond after that, but I was okay with the interaction. I needed to feel wanted and beautiful, and he gave it to me. So, I was satisfied with his response. I removed my dress and lay on the empty bed alone.

The next morning, Carlos seemed carefree. But, on that day, I knew I would cheat again.

"Did you ask Carlos about that night?" Kendra asked.

"No, what was the point?"

"So, how often did you speak to Chris?"

"We didn't speak over the phone. Chris had his life, and so did I. We would text each other daily but kept in-person visits minimal."

I continued explaining how I was soaking in the compliments that Chris was feeding my ego. My ego provided my confidence, which gave me the energy to work out even more. It was like I was taking drugs and enjoying that high, and I kept returning for more. At this point, it just complimented and flirted for months.

Several weeks passed, and I received the news that Carlos's father was coming into town. I was surprised because we had not seen him for about seven years.

"How long will he be here?" I asked Carlos.

"Does it matter?"

That was the wrong question to ask, but I needed to know. The last time my father-in-law lived with us wasn't great, and Carlos and I already had issues he ignored. So, as I waited for his response, I looked at him.

"Is he coming on a one-way ticket?"

There was no way our living arrangements were going to work out. We lived in a 700-square-foot one-bedroom apartment. Carlos and I slept in the bedroom while his father slept on an air mattress in the living room. For access to our bathroom, he had to enter our bedroom whenever he needed to use it.

While Carlos was at work, I was at home with his father. It was always uncomfortable for me to be alone with men, let alone with his dad. So, watching TV in the living room one day, I got up and walked outside to take my fur baby for a walk. In anticipation of going to sleep, my father-in-law turned off the TV and the living room light. But, instead, he sent me to bed before I finished watching the show.

Even though I was upset, I didn't say anything and walked to my room. The same night, when Carlos got home, I knew I had to tell him what had happened. Since his father was in the next room, I calmly approached the conversation. During our conversation, I explained what happened and how I felt about it.

Carlos looked straight at me and said, "Oh well, deal with it."

"Okay, I'll deal with it." I went to bed, upset.

A few weeks later, I moved out.

"Do you think this was the best way to handle the situation?" Kendra asked.

"It was the hardest decision I ever made, but he gave me no other choice."

When I moved into my place, I was sick to my stomach. I hadn't lived on my own for eleven years. I wasn't sure if I could afford this apartment alone, but I didn't want to allow him to continue treating me like shit, especially when I was the only one who cared for Carlos for so long. Because I've done it before, I know how to build myself up from nothing. So, during my first few weeks, I slept on the carpet.

"Did Carlos look for you?"

"No."

I was angry because he didn't put up a fight for me at all. Before I moved out, I told him my plan. He had no care in the world. So, when I finally moved out, I felt he didn't care since he didn't look for me. I cried for weeks in an empty apartment. I cried like a tiny baby, wondering what I had done to deserve all this type of punishment. Once again, I was all alone and did what I knew to do: self-isolate.

"Was Chris aware of your move?" she asked.

"Chris found out weeks later," I responded.

I promised myself I wouldn't see him again. However, this separation required me to deal with my own emotions. While I didn't want to divorce Carlos, I wanted him to wake up. At this point, I felt like Carlos was only with me because he needed me, not because he wanted me. In other words, he was proving me right.

"How are you feeling?" Chris sounded genuinely concerned for me.

"I feel lonely and sad," I started explaining

"Why? Your husband was an asshole. If you get back with him, you would be stupid."

I sat quietly, listening to his little rant.

"I thought you were smarter than that to consider giving him another chance. Don't be an idiot."

His comment stunned me. We discussed why we were unhappy in our relationship and what our spouses were doing to us. I told him a lot, but I didn't think he would throw it in my face as he did. I didn't feel any compassion from him at all. I quickly shut down, but he wanted to have sex, and I didn't put up a fight about it. I gave my body to him, and once he left, I felt disgusted.

"What triggered you to shut down, Janell?" Kendra asked.

"It reminded me of my mother when he said he thought I was smarter than that."

He spoke to me so sternly as if he had authority over me. The friendship we had before started to change. He started calling me more, and if I didn't answer, he would question me.

I didn't have anything in my apartment, so Chris gave me some money. Although I did not wish to accept it, he effectively made me feel supported. I didn't realize it was all a trap. The Chris I knew before seemed to shift into a different person. He certainly wasn't interested in hearing what I had to say about Carlos but would want me to listen to his issues.

He would call me to vent about an argument between him and his wife. I would naturally provide my opinion.

"You have provided for her all these years, and she is comfortable with a certain lifestyle. Now you have to deal with it," I said.

"What the fuck do you mean?" Chris asked.

"You can't expect her to do for you when you have spoiled her."

"You don't know what the fuck you are talking about, Janell. Plus, who the fuck are you to talk about my situation when you let Carlos walk all over you."

When he was upset, he spoke in such a negative way to make himself feel superior. After observing him act the same way toward me as he would toward everyone else, I gradually distanced myself. I occasionally believed what he said after he belittled me. When we argued, he would hang up the phone and not speak to me for days, making me feel sick. Sometimes, it would be months before I saw him again, and I was fine after a few days. Then he would come around again, and I would fall. Then the cycle continued.

What was happening didn't make sense to me. I knew Chris wasn't suitable for me, but I would suffer through withdrawals from him.

As a result, he was able to manipulate my mind. Around him, I felt weak. While he knew how to love me, he also knew how to punish me with it. As a result, I lacked affection and love, which he fed me, causing me to behave differently.

Then when he wanted to have sex, he would show up at my apartment, and I didn't know how to say no. So, every time that occurred, I cried and was angry at myself.

As a result, I started drinking, which sometimes got out of hand. I drank so much that I vomited my guts out, but that didn't stop me from getting drunk. There were times when I would get drunk and drive. I didn't care about life. I was depressed. My husband didn't want me, I was struggling with my business, I was about to lose my car, and Chris treated me like shit. It exhausted me, and I didn't know what I had done wrong to put myself in such a bind. I've even contemplated taking my own life several times.

"Do you think the relationship, personally and professionally, with Chris is worth this torture?" Kendra asked.

"No," I responded without hesitation.

"Then leave him alone."

"I'm trying."

As my life coach suggested, I should ask for a divorce to handle myself and get better without him being aware of the struggles I needed to heal from alone. Plus, I didn't know what he could do, and I wanted to avoid that from happening. He did know I suffered from depression and anxiety because of my diagnosis of PCOS.

As a result, whenever Carlos saw me upset or emotional, I would blame my PCOS. I was not willing to tell him about the horrendous situation I was in with someone who exploited my vulnerability and my lack of self-worth.

According to my life coach, what he did was emotional abuse. It was apparent to him what I was missing, and he used it against me every time. Due to the depression, I felt that leaving our home made me prone to emotional abuse.

How could I tell Carlos? I don't want to blame anyone but myself. As a grown woman, I should have known better, but just as Carlos was sick and addicted to his pills, I guess I was sick and addicted to toxic behavior.

As a result, I distanced myself from Carlos, so the toxic energy I was producing wouldn't affect him. I hoped for a divorce. I told Carlos I was dating other people, which wasn't entirely true, but I didn't know how to tell him a guy was manipulating me. Chris was my punishment for cheating on Carlos, and I needed to figure out how to stop it.

Over three years, this situation came and went. Eventually, I was able to get away from Chris and cut all ties personally with the help of counseling. However, I did maintain the professional side of it because I was mentally healthy at this point, and anything he said or did no longer affected me. He tried plenty of times, and I was very cold-hearted toward him. I don't dislike him for what he did to me, but I know I regret meeting him.

Despite getting into a comfortable place, I sometimes couldn't face Carlos. Because I felt guilty, I tried to maintain a friendship with him. I wanted Carlos to want me sexually. Now that he was showing interest, I felt my body was so filthy with the touch of another man that I couldn't bear to give it back to him. At this point, I felt unworthy of his touch.

But be careful what you feed into the universe. It might come to fruition sooner than expected.

CHAPTER 18

YOU ARE NOT ALONE

Have you ever felt alone, even in the presence of another person?

It didn't occur to me that someone was nearby with similar experiences. But unfortunately, staying strong and being afraid to speak about mental illness is common, so we don't know what others are going through.

Rosa is a mother of two who struggles with caring for her husband, who suffers from a brain injury. I was interested in speaking with her about this subject, and she accepted.

"Thank you for taking the time to discuss this with me," I said.

Our conversation started naturally, so we both felt comfortable. Briefly, I shared my story and struggles. Rosa was ready to speak and gave me details about her husband's story.

"When Bob was nine, he suffered a severe head injury in a car accident. Despite rescuers reviving him, he suffered short-term memory loss and a chemical imbalance in his brain."

"Oh wow," I said.

"Since Bob was a kid, he's always been on medications for depression and anxiety. Later in life, he received a diagnosis of PTSD, insomnia, and OCD."

Like Carlos and I, Rosa and Bob have long-term relationships. In addition, Carlos and Bob both suffered injuries which made Rosa and I caregivers. Putting that connection together had me even more intrigued.

"I know how difficult it is being a caregiver to your loved one. But do you ever feel resentful toward your husband?" I asked.

"There have been times when I felt those feelings. I feel like on certain occasions, such as being sick. I wanted to be taken care of, but I still have to take care of him and our household."

I checked out helpguide.com (2022) to learn more about caregivers' feelings. The following are common signs and symptoms of caregiver stress:

1. Anxiety, depression, irritability
2. Feeling tired and run down
3. Difficulty sleeping
4. Overreacting to minor nuisances
5. New or worsening health problems

6. Trouble concentrating
7. Feeling increasingly resentful
8. Drinking, smoking, or eating more
9. Neglecting responsibilities
10. Cutting back on leisure activities

I experienced every symptom on the list. So, the next question will be, "How can we overcome these symptoms?"

While researching the answer to this question, I felt such anxiety. The anxiety built because I knew these answers were easier said or written than being able to complete them. For example, they suggested that a busy caregiver take some leisure time. The caregiver owes themselves to schedule some rest or does things for themselves. These were also the suggested focuses by helpguide.com (2022):

1. Maintain your relationships
2. Share your feelings
3. Prioritize activities that bring your enjoyment
4. Find ways to pamper yourself
5. Make yourself laugh
6. Get out of the house

These all sound great, but how does a person do these things without the guilt or the worry that while you are out enjoying yourself, your loved one isn't back home trying to kill themselves? How do you get out of your fucking head and not feel the guilt that you are out enjoying yourself and they are at home suffering?

As I wrote this part of the book, I felt anger. I appreciate all the suggestions, but did they come from someone who has gone through what Rosa and I have? My experience will help me address these suggestions.

> **Maintain your relationships**—People have pushed you away because you need to handle what's happening in your home. If you are trying to maintain your relationships, the smiles on your face are fake. We are putting up a facade. As a result of my husband's comments or advances toward my family or friends, my personal relationship almost ended.

Examples:

   a. When Carlos abused his pills, he also sold them to those who would pay good money. A friend of mine wanted a pill, and he told her he would give it to her if she showed him her breasts.
   b. Also, Carlos had a different relationship with my sister. She would confide in him more than I at that time. He gave her advice and told her that if we weren't related, he would have hooked up with her.
   c. The most recent situation I was aware of was his conversation with my assistant, Desi. They were speaking about marijuana, and he told her he didn't like smoking a certain kind because it made him horny.

They didn't want to tell me in each of these instances because they felt uncomfortable. They knew I would also have a hard time with it. But these moments are embarrassing and would have caused me to shy away from others so I wouldn't look like a fool.

Share your feelings—News flash, many people don't care. At least, that's how we feel. If we share any vulnerability, we are weak. People who have no clue or never experienced the shit we go through tell us what to do and what not to do. Also, you can share your feelings with those in your circle, but they will need help understanding. For example, his mother knew the circumstances since she would spend some weeks in the summer with us. I would also express myself to her, but she suggested he drank cough medicine when he had trouble sleeping. I found him passed out because he mixed cough medicine with sprint and drank it like a celebratory drink.

Prioritize activities that bring your enjoyment—Like what? Look back at chapter "Discharge," where I spoke about going on vacation with my friends because I needed it. What mess did I have to come back and have to solve? Carlos drove while high and crashed our pickup truck. I didn't have anyone to take care of Carlos while I was gone, but his sister came from Tampa to assist, so what happened? She passed judgment on me based on the information provided by Carlos. I couldn't share my feelings because that was his sister who was on his side without the full knowledge of his mental illness. Why is that? Because mental illness is such a secret topic to discuss.

His sister and I didn't speak for a long time. I chose that for myself because I was upset that instead of her asking me what was happening, she decided that whatever Carlos told her was the truth. To this day, I don't know what story he created, but I know it caused more issues in our relationship. I started to look at Carlos differently because if he was so evil to have someone turn against me, why was I dealing with this mess?

Find ways to pamper yourself—How is this possible when there are limited funds, especially for those with only one income? With Carlos and I, for example, I was the sole breadwinner for many years. I had to consider the expenses for both of us, not just myself. Also, Carlos had a spending habit and needed to learn how to control money. There were many fights because of finances.

Make yourself laugh—How? If we are consistently thinking of an illness. How can we find humor in that? Let me think about it hard. I sure did laugh, but it was more of that evil laugh. More of that anger laugh toward the world toward Carlos. The laughter changes you internally. How can you turn back from any of these situations I've faced?

Get out of the house—The only time I could get out without feeling guilty was to walk my dog or run. I would wake up, and before I ate, I would go outside to run. Living in Orlando, I needed to wake up early enough to avoid the hottest sun, which was difficult.

My diagnosis made it very difficult to wake up before 8 a.m.

As I continued speaking with Rosa, I found another similarity between us.

"I also have PCOS," Rosa said.

Carlos's injury, mental illness, and issues have always been top priorities, so my mental conditions were unimportant. However, I did want to figure out why my weight would yo-yo. Why I was growing hair on my upper lip and chin, wouldn't get my period for months or even years, had mood issues, never got pregnant, and had issues sleeping and waking up. I had so many issues with my body, but from lack of funds, it was hard to seek help.

It wasn't until I went to an ob-gyn that had experience with PCOS that they listened to all my issues. Then, they requested I do blood work and return to the office for a follow-up.

I sat waiting in the office, looking around at the posters of the woman's anatomy. Then, finally, the doctor walked into the office and looked straight at her waiting for the results.

"Mrs. Peña, we looked over your test results. They were not normal." Dr. Martinez said. She continued asking me, "Did you fast before taking the blood work as instructed?"

"Yes, I did fast," I responded.

"In addition to insulin resistance, I suspect you have PCOS based on your other symptoms." Dr. Martinez stated. She continued explaining that she wanted to conduct one more examination before she gave me that diagnosis. Then, they requested an ultrasound of my uterus. I lay on that bed, waiting for the technician to enter the room.

"Mrs. Peña we'll ultrasound your uterus, inserting a wand in your vagina," she said.

I just laid back and looked straight at the screen. My next step was to learn what the technician was looking for on the screen. So, I didn't ask any questions.

"Please get dressed, and the doctor will be with you shortly."

Dr. Martinez walked into the room and stated, "The ultrasound showed that you have a cyst on your ovaries."

The doctor explained that I have polycystic ovary syndrome. At this point, I was already thirty-six years old. To me, it meant I would never have kids with this condition. I thought the worst. I think about anything else or any of the other symptoms or issues that come with PCOS. The doctor assured me I could have kids in the future, but it would be difficult because of my age and my condition.

I left that office in tears. I drove to the East Coast toward the water, knowing it would bring me peace. At that point, my diagnosis made me think of myself first before anyone else. I honestly didn't know of anyone else but me.

I walked the bridge over the water back and forth several times and just cried. I was wondering if I was ever okay with not having a child.

I started to think maybe God didn't want me to have any kids because Carlos was too unstable to raise a child with me.

I also started thinking that maybe what my mother did to me I would reflect on my child, so God didn't want that to happen.

Let me explain some of the complications that come along with PCOS (2022):

- Infertility
- Gestational diabetes or pregnancy-induced high blood pressure
- Miscarriage or premature birth
- Nonalcoholic steatohepatitis—a severe liver inflammation caused by fat accumulation in the liver
- Metabolic syndrome—a cluster of conditions including high blood pressure, high blood sugar, and abnormal cholesterol or triglyceride levels that significantly increase your risk of cardiovascular disease
- Type 2 diabetes or prediabetes
- Sleep apnea
- Depression, anxiety, and eating disorders
- Abnormal uterine bleeding
- Cancer of the uterine lining (endometrial cancer)

Yes, this condition is a chronic illness which sounds very scary. Since this book is about mental health, I want to expand on the fact that one of the complications is depression, anxiety, and eating disorders. Yup, I had mental disorders, which all made sense now. I didn't have time to be depressed, but depression wasn't just sad for yourself. The following are other signs of depression stated by verywellhealth.com (Grassi 2022):

- Fatigue
- Sadness
- Loneliness
- Helplessness
- Tearfulness
- Sleep disturbances
- Lack of motivation
- Appetite changes
- Changes in weight (this is also a sign of PCOS itself)
- Feelings of guilt
- Difficulty concentrating
- Loss of interest in sex
- Loss of interest in hobbies or activities previously enjoyed
- Poor decision-making
- Headaches
- Physical pains such as neck or backache
- Digestive issues

Out of fifteen on the list, I had fourteen. The loss of interest in sex was the only one I wasn't lacking. As I continued researching PCOS, I realized I needed to put myself first. If I don't take care of myself, I won't be good to anyone else.

I texted Janina, the staff from the high school who also has PCOS, to ask her if she remembered my situation and if she would like to share how she felt. She responded quickly to my request. The following are her words:

Behind closed doors, you stayed focused and determined, and you stuck it out. You stayed on the course and have overcome much more than you or anyone else thought. You are one successful woman. Someone else may not have that opportunity, but it was you and your determination all these years.

These words help me remember my type of person and who I've always been. No matter what I go through, I will overcome it all. No matter how hard you try to break me, I will cry it out, dust it off, and get back up again.

CHAPTER 19

THE FINAL CHAPTER

As much as I hate to admit it, I am guilty of what most people do in life.

As I sit here and write this final chapter, I reflect on everything I've written and notice I could have done better. I've talked so much about the problems that I missed so many instances of the good. There were a lot of positive things that happened, but I didn't explain many of them.

We all know that we cannot just divorce our parents, but it is easier to divorce our spouses. After all I have been through, you may wonder why I have stayed so long. Wouldn't it have been better if I had walked out sooner?

I've done many things throughout the years to try and get into a positive place for myself, but I couldn't have written this book without being honest about everything.

When I heard the words of our divorce over the phone, I felt destroyed. I couldn't believe what was about to happen also, that Carlos couldn't even give me the respect to say this all to my face. After seventeen years of being in his life, I deserved him to sit with me and talk like an adult. He didn't give me that at all, so I knew he didn't care about how I felt.

I ask myself many questions all the time. It was a tough decision for me, but I'm glad Carlos made it for us. Yes, I cried for several days straight. Then I wept on and off for several weeks. Then I broke down when memories came flooding back.

After months of crying, feeling anger, sadness, and depression, I realized divorce was the best decision he ever made for us. I still felt anger toward him because he didn't give me the divorce when I asked for it, but when he felt like giving it to me. In a way, I felt like that was his way of holding on and maybe trying to fix us, so I waited. I waited for years for him to get himself together. Finally, he asked, "Why did it take you so long to seek help?" He had no clue or even remembered me seeking help.

Finally, I blocked him from all my social media pages and cell phone. But I didn't stop there. I deleted his side of the family. I didn't want to see them enjoying their life since I was no longer a family member. Let's face it, they say things will not change, but it already has for me.

It was easy for him to divorce me, and now the individuals who were not there through his darkest moments get to enjoy him at his finest. Knowing this is a struggle for me, but I know that walking out of his life the first time kept him alive. Even today, he is striving to be a better individual. Now that I know my purpose in his life was to keep him alive, I am grateful.

Trying to reflect on great memories, I made a phone call to his older sister Yanaira. I wanted to know if she could remind me of some good moments or anything she could remember Carlos doing that showed he loved me.

"Janell, I can't recall many moments, but one that sticks out is when he made sure we had healthy food at family gatherings. He wanted to ensure you didn't feel guilty for eating unhealthily."

I stood quiet because those were moments I wasn't aware of when it happened. Despite all the craziness, there was love between us. Whenever he was himself, he exhibited a sense of caring.

The first year Carlos and I separated, the family came into town. Some stayed in my apartment, and some stayed with him in his. I was so emotional because the sense of family was back together, but Carlos and I were not. Dealing with it all was so emotional, but I didn't want it to end. We all went to Magic Kingdom, and with the heat, walking, and hunger, everyone was getting on each other's nerves. Carlos and I stood back and watched everyone yell at each other. I looked over and saw ice cream.

"Carlos, let's gets some ice cream."

"Let's go," he said with a big smile.

We walked over and stood in line. We faced each other. "We are the separated ones, and we should be fighting, and yet here we are about to eat ice cream."

He put his arms around me, and I laid my face into his chest and my arms around his waist. At this moment, I felt the safest I had felt for so long that I just started crying. Then, I felt him kissing the top of my head.

We hugged, and I cried in front of everyone. Then the family stopped arguing, walked over, and didn't say anything but got some ice cream with us. All you could hear from then on was laughter and fun.

Moments like these are the moments that made me stay. Carlos was home for me. He was my comfort zone. Carlos has a big heart and would give a person his last dollar if needed. I had to remember what his psychologist would tell me. "Janell, when Carlos is in a manic stage, he will do things he will not recall doing. It isn't him but his illness."

There were times I couldn't excuse his behavior, but I loved him so much that I couldn't just fully let him go. He would drop anything to help me, no matter where I was or with whom. For example, I had an important exam with the IRS one morning, but my car decided not to start for some reason. I called Carlos in a panic and was freaking out because I needed to be there on time. He raced to me to give me a jump with no questions.

He was a very romantic gentleman. He would randomly bring me flowers, and it didn't even need to be a memorable holiday. He would give me heartfelt postcards on special holidays with words of his love for me. He is also one to jump out of the car to pump my gas. He would even open every door for me. When he was out shopping, it was scarce that he wouldn't buy me something. He always thought about me, even in the little moments.

He was remarkable when he was himself and not struggling through any stages of his illness. Very thoughtful and caring. There was a time when I was sick before COVID-19 ever existed. I had to go to work because I supported us and couldn't afford to call off. When I got home, Carlos cooked homemade chicken soup to help me feel better. Just to let you know, he was no chef. Carlos called our chef friend to ask how to make the soup. It was his goal to make sure I liked the soup, but most importantly, it would make me feel better.

I know he felt I didn't appreciate anything he ever did for me, but honestly, I enjoyed everything. It was hard for me to show him those emotions because I expected something to go bad. I had to prepare myself for another disappointment. It was the same disappointment I felt with my mother. I experienced her good days and her bad days. I knew my mother wasn't horrible, but her untreated illness drove her to do irrational things. I knew that a day would come when I would have to put up with some type of mess.

So, on January 20, 2022, I called Carlos after I came home from work. I knew he was out in West Palm Beach, where he would usually go and disappear. I never knew the reason for his disappearance act, but we women have that woman's intuition when something isn't right.

"Hello," Carlos answered.

"Are you still down there?" Since we had planned to go out for dinner that same night.

"Yes."

I paused with a lump in my throat. He heard it.

"Why?"

"Well, you knew I had a doctor's appointment today and didn't even ask how it went."

"Did you ask me how I'm doing?"

He caught me by surprise by asking that question. He knew I recently went to the specialist to find out if we could get pregnant. But unfortunately, his actions made it seem like he didn't care for the process.

I questioned myself for a second if I should have asked him how he was feeling.

During our argument, Carlos decided to break the news to me. He dropped a major bomb on me that, to this day, I can't forget the words that came out of his mouth. He wanted to end our relationship, and the following were his reasons.

"I feel like you are not genuine and are scared of my growth. I feel like you are trying to have a baby just to keep me. We have no true connection. I don't think I can take you on the next journey of my life. I can't be with someone just because I feel obligated to them."

These are words that keep replaying in my head. How can he think so negatively of me after all these years? It was a hurt that I had never felt or even could comprehend.

I shouted out in tears while unable to breathe, "How can you do this to me? How can you take everything away from me in just one night? This is what I always feared. You are taking away my husband, best friend, and family in seconds."

I cried uncontrollably, which was the first time I ever showed those emotions toward him. I felt him go through the phone and just rip my heart out of my chest. He not only crushed it but also placed it in acid, so I could never feel again.

Even after he hurt me, I had to call him to ensure he was okay. I knew he was driving while we had this conversation, so I wanted to ensure he didn't have an accident and made it home safely. He did answer the phone and told me he was sleeping and made it home okay. That's when I knew he didn't care. I was up all night, and he was okay with my hurt as he slept as if nothing had happened.

The next day I couldn't even cry. I was still in shock, trying to process the information. My assistant, Desi, came over to be by my side while I went through my emotions. I couldn't believe that as much as I cared for him and tried never to intentionally hurt his feelings throughout the years, he could say such hurtful things to me.

To me, of all people. The person there for him through his worst. So, I spoke to the counselor I had at the time and explained what had happened. She was shocked because she had encouraged me to show him the love and affection that I didn't show throughout the last years of our relationship.

She encouraged me not to let his last words bother me because we knew it wasn't true. Those words were not a reflection of me, but he would need to say something to hurt me, ultimately pushing me away. However, she did state for me to write the opposite of those words or the words I wished for him to say that would have ended our relationship on better terms.

You are one of the most genuine individuals I know, and I just don't want to hurt you while I find myself.
Or
You have helped me grow into who I am today, and I will forever be grateful.
Or
Although I would have loved to have a baby with you, I feel like it isn't the right time for me, and I don't want to hold you back from seeking a family.
Or
Our connection is different, but I would love to experience other connections.

> *Or*
> *You have been a part of my journey throughout all these years, and I am sorry that most of them have been negative. I want to let you go so you can experience a positive journey.*
> *Or*
> *I appreciate everything you have ever done for me in these seventeen years of our lives, and there isn't anything I can do to change what has happened but to let you go to find your happiness.*

These were the words I preferred to hear from someone I truly loved and thought truly loved me in return.

Several weeks later, I discovered he was already in a relationship with someone else. He was in this relationship for about seven months before ending ours. That hurt even more. I realized he meant every single word because, as someone with borderline personality disorder, Carlos can devalue someone so quickly.

My sister spoke to him, and the only words I remember him telling her were, "It was seventeen years of my life I can't get back."

That was it. There was nothing left of me in Carlos's heart or mind. So, the next journey in my life is to focus on myself and my healing.

ACKNOWLEDGMENTS

Writing a book is harder than I thought and more rewarding than I could have ever imagined. None of this would have been possible without my inner circle being there for me during these challenging times. Without you ladies, Elynel, Elyahna, Elena, Desiree, Nina, Iris, Vani, and Amanda, I may not have survived. You are my forever family. The love I have for you will be forever.

Mom, thank you for giving me lessons that helped me endure many obstacles in my life. You gave me the smart gene, and I'll forever be grateful.

My sister, Amanda, thank you for helping us build a stronger sister bond, but you will forever be my child.

To my assistant, Desi, thank you for keeping the business flowing when I wanted to give it up and tracking my money when I wanted to go on a spending spree. Thank you because we survived it.

Nana, thank you for encouraging me to have a hot girl summer, and Nina, for being my partner in crime.

To my extended family, Carmen, thank you for being that mother figure to me for so many years of my life. Yana, thank you for being a sister and my friend. Thank you for giving me a place in the kid's hearts. I will be forever grateful for all these years.

Carlos, thank you for helping me become the woman I am today. Thank you for all the good memories we've shared in our journey together and for allowing us to experience a different one.

To all the individuals who had faith in me and preordered this book, I want to thank you! Thank you to Melva, Olga, Eladio, Ricardo, Gisell, Shelly, Damaris, Demerise, Amanda, Elena, Judi, Gene, Vanessa F., Nancy, Eric, Janina, Iris, Wolf, LG, Melonie, Francisco, Ivelisse, Stephanie, Carymar, Enelise, and Jeanette. Your support made this possible.

Additionally, my special thanks to Julio, my biggest supporter. Although this period of my life had many ups and downs, God placed you in my path at the right time. I am ready for our journey. Thank you!

Finally, thank you to my little fur babies. Dulce, my little fur angel, stood by our side through our entire journey. Thank you! Bam Bam, for being my little rock. You made sure Mommy did not stay in bed for too long. Thank you!

APPENDIX

CHAPTER 1

Labossiere, Stephan. 2019. *Love After Heartbreak: Volume 1.* United States: Highly Favored Publishing LLC.

National Alliance of Mental Health. n.d. "Mental Health by the Numbers | NAMI: National Alliance on Mental Illness." National Alliance of Mental Illness. Accessed October 3, 2022. https://www.nami.org/mhstats.

National Alliance of Mental Health. n.d. "Mental Health Conditions | NAMI: National Alliance on Mental Illness." National Alliance of Mental Illness. Accessed October 3, 2022. https://www.nami.org/About-Mental-Illness/Mental-Health-Conditions.

CHAPTER 9

Toone, Stephanie. 2020. "Family is powerless | Kim Kardashian makes statement on Kanye West's mental health." *The Atlanta Journal—Constitution.* July 22, 2020. https://www.ajc.com/ (accessed October 3, 2022).

CHAPTER 12

Cherry, Kendra. 2022. "8 Signs You're an Introvert." *Psychology* (blog), *Very Well Mind*. May 13, 2022. https://www.verywellmind.com/signs-you-are-an-introvert-2795427.

CHAPTER 18

Grassi, Angela. 2022. "PCOS and Depression." *Health A–Z* (blog), *Very Well Health*. March 23, 2022. https://www.verywellhealth.com/pcos-depression-4014178.

Mayo Clinic Staff. "Polycystic Ovary Syndrome (PCOS)." *Patient Care and Health Information* (blog), Mayo Clinic. September 08, 2022. https://www.mayoclinic.org/diseases-conditions/pcos/symptoms-causes/syc-20353439.

Smith, Melina. 2022. "Caregiver Stress and Burnout." *Family Caregiving* (blog), *Help Guide.* November 1, 2022. https://www.helpguide.org/articles/stress/caregiver-stress-and-burnout.htm#:~:text=Common%20signs%20and%20symptoms%20of,Difficulty%20sleeping.

www.ingramcontent.com/pod-product-compliance
Lightning Source LLC
LaVergne TN
LVHW012016060526
838201LV00061B/4336